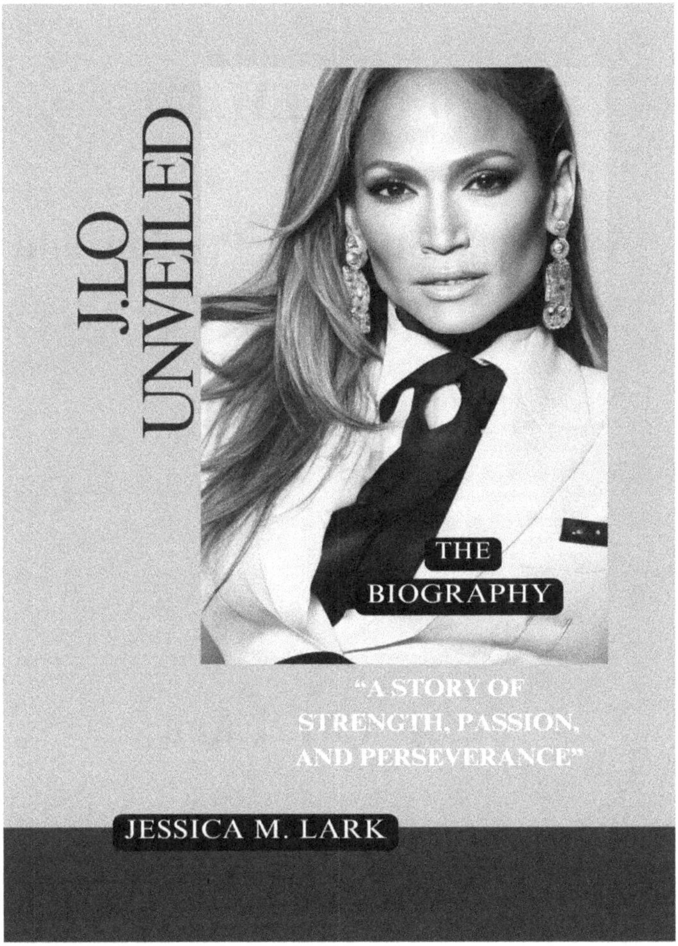

J.LO
UNVEILED

THE
BIOGRAPHY

"A STORY OF
STRENGTH, PASSION,
AND PERSEVERANCE"

JESSICA M. LARK

J.Lo UNVEILED

"A Story of Strength, Passion, and Perseverance"

By

Jessica M. Lark

All rights reserved. No part of this publication may be reproduced, distributed, or transmitted in any form or by any means, including photocopying, recording, or other electronic or mechanical methods, without the prior written permission of the publisher, except in the case of brief quotations embodied in critical reviews and certain other noncommercial uses permitted by copyright law.
Copyright © Jessica M. Lark, 2023

Table Of Content

Introduction

Welcome to the enthralling world of "J.Lo UNVEILED: "A Story of Strength, Passion, and Perseverance". Within these pages, you will embark on a witching trip through the life and triumphs of a global icon. This strictly drafted memoir not only chronicles the mileposts of Jennifer Lopez's extraordinary career but delves into the substance of her adaptability, art, and insuperable spirit. Get ready to discover the innumerous stories behind the limelight, as we unravel the layers of an unequaled heritage that continues to shape the realms of music, film, and fashion. Enjoy the Odyssey through the lens of one of the most influential numbers of our time.

CHAPTER 1

EARLY LIFE AND FAMILY BACKGROUND

Jennifer Lopez, born on July 24, 1969, in the Bronx, New York City, is a famed American actress, songster, cotillion, and businesswoman. She was raised in a close-knit Puerto Rican family, and her early life gests significantly shaped her multifaceted career.

Lopez's parents, Guadalupe Rodríguez and David Lopez, instilled a strong work heritage and perseverance in their three daughters, Jennifer being the middle child.

Her father worked at a computer establishment, and her mama was a kindergarten school teacher, furnishing a stable and probative terrain for their family.

From a youthful age, Jennifer displayed a passion for entertainment. She started taking cotillion assignments at the age of five and shared in colorful academy products. Her parents honored her gift and enrolled her in singing and acting classes, fostering her cultural development.

Growing up in the Bronx during the 1970s and 1980s, a time marked by profitable challenges and social metamorphoses, had a profound impact on Lopez. The neighborhood's rich artistic diversity told her music and cotillion style, incorporating rudiments of Latin, hipsterism- hop, and R&B into her after performances.

After graduating from Preston High School, Lopez attended Baruch College for a short period but soon decided to pursue her true passion for performing. She joined cotillion groups and worked as a backup cotillion for artists like New Kids on the Block and Janet Jackson. This early experience laid the foundation for her unborn success in the entertainment industry.

Jennifer's advance came in 1991 when she earned a spot as a" Fly Girl" cotillion on the TV show" In Living Color." This occasion exposed her to a broader followership and opened doors for acting places. Her determination led her to secure her first major acting part in the film" My Family"(1995).

In 1999, Jennifer Lopez released her debut reader," On the 6," which featured hit mates like" If You Had My Love" and" Waiting for Tonight." This marked the morning of her successful music career, completing her thriving amusement trials.

Beyond her professional achievements, Lopez's particular life has frequently been in the public eye. Her marriages to Ojani Noa, Cris Judd, and Marc Anthony, as well as high- profile connections with numbers like Sean Combs and Ben

Affleck, have contributed to her celebrity status.

In conclusion, Jennifer Lopez's early life and family background laid the root for her remarkable career. From the vibrant thoroughfares of the Bronx to global stardom, her trip reflects adaptability, gift, and a grim pursuit of her passion.

Cultural Influences in Jennifer Lopez's Upbringing

Jennifer Lopez's parenting is deeply embedded in a rich shade of artistic influences that have played a vital part in shaping her identity and contributing to the dynamic artist we know at the moment. Her artistic heritage has been a significant source of alleviation throughout her life.

Growing up in a generally Hispanic community in the Bronx, Jennifer was immersed in the vibrant and different shade of Latin American culture. Her parents, proud of their Puerto Rican roots, instilled a strong sense of artistic pride in their three daughters, fostering a deep connection to their heritage. Traditional music, cotillion , and cookery were integral corridors of the Lopez ménage, furnishing Jennifer with a foundation that would later impact her cultural expressions.

The music of Puerto Rico, ranging from salsa to merengue, came as a soundtrack to Jennifer's constructive times. Her exposure to these metrical beats and lively warbles set up its way into her early passion for cotillion . This artistic infusion, combined with the civic sounds of hipsterism- hop and R&B currently in the Bronx during the 1970s and 1980s, laid the root for the miscellaneous emulsion that defines Lopez's musical style.

The significance of family and community is a recreating theme in Hispanic societies, and it resonates deeply in Jennifer Lopez's life. Raised in a tight- knit family, she frequently speaks about the influence of her parents and sisters, who inclusively

14

created a probative terrain that nurtured her dreams. The value of hard work and determination, instilled by her parents, came from guiding principles that propelled her to success in the entertainment industry.

In addition to her Puerto Rican heritage, Jennifer's parenting was also shaped by the civic culture of the Bronx. The city's artistic melting pot exposed her to a variety of influences, contributing to her versatility as an artist. The graffiti-covered thoroughfares, the metrical sounds of the neighborhood, and the adaptability of its people all left an unforgettable mark on her cultural sensibilities.

Beyond her particular guests , Jennifer Lopez has constantly used her platform to celebrate and amplify Latinx voices in the entertainment industry. From incorporating Latin measures into her music to laboriously sharing in systems that showcase Latinx stories, she has become a prominent advocate for artistic representation.

In conclusion, the artistic influences in Jennifer Lopez's parenting are a mosaic of Puerto Rican heritage, Bronx civic life, and a profound appreciation for the diversity that shaped her. These influences haven't only amended her particular life but have also come integral rudiments of her cultural expression, contributing to her status as a global icon in the world of entertainment.

CHAPTER 2

THE RISE FROM THE BRONS

Jennifer Lopez's rise from the Bronx is a testament to her tenacity, gift, and determination to overcome challenges in pursuit of her dreams. Lopez surfaced from a community that, during the late 20th century, faced profitable rigors, social struggles, and was frequently overshadowed by negative conceptions.

Growing up in a working- class Puerto Rican family, Lopez's parents, Guadalupe Rodríguez and David Lopez, instilled in her a strong work heritage and adaptability. The Bronx, though scuffling with adversity, handed a rich ground for the development of her artistic identity and cultural bourne . The city's vibrant blend of Latin, African- American, and Caribbean influences came as the background for Lopez's trip to stardom.

Lopez's early guests in the Bronx burned her passion for entertainment. She attended Preston High School, where she continued to hone her chops in singing and dancing. Her intentions led her to Manhattan, where she started taking cotillion classes and worked as a backup cotillion for colorful artists, laying the foundation for her future career.

The breakthrough moment came when Lopez secured a spot as a" Fly Girl" cotillion on the megahit TV show" In Living Color" in 1991. This occasion not only showcased her cotillion prowess but also exposed her to a wider followership. It marked a pivotal turning point, opening doors for acting places in TV and film.

In 1995, Jennifer Lopez landed a commanding part in the film" Selena," portraying the iconic Tejano songster Selena Quintanilla- Pérez. The performance garnered wide sun, establishing Lopez as a talented actress and pelting her into the limelight. Her trip from the Bronx to Hollywood challenged prevailing sundries and came as an alleviation for aspiring artists from underrepresented backgrounds.

Resemblant to her acting success, Lopez ventured into the music industry. In 1999, she released her debut reader," On the 6," featuring map-beat successes like" If You Had My Love." The reader's success solidified her status as a multifaceted imitator, seamlessly blending pop, Latin, and R&B influences.

Jennifer Lopez's rise from the Bronx embodies the spirit of adaptability and determination. Her success not only shattered conceptions associated with her background but also paved the way for lesser diversity and representation in the entertainment industry. Beyond her individual achievements, Lopez remains connected to her roots, using her platform to celebrate and hoist the Bronx, showcasing it as a source of alleviation and strength.

In conclusion, Jennifer Lopez's trip from the Bronx to global stardom is a compelling narrative of triumph over adversity. It underscores the transformative power of gift, hard work, and a grim pursuit of one's passion, leaving an unforgettable mark on the entertainment geography and inspiring generations to come.

Navigating Challenges

Navigating challenges has been a recreating theme in Jennifer Lopez's outstanding career, reflecting her adaptability, rigidity, and unwavering determination to overcome obstacles. From early struggles in the entertainment assiduity to balancing a multifaceted career, Lopez's trip is a testament to her capability to defy and triumph over challenges.

And rejection, particularly in the film industry. Despite her gift, being a Latina actress posed challenges in an assiduity that, at the time, had limited openings for diversity. Still, Lopez persisted, landing advanced places that defied conceptions and showcased her amusement prowess. Her determination to navigate the hurdles of typecasting and artistic impulses paved the way for lesser inclusivity in Hollywood.

Balancing her places as a songster, actress, and cotillion presented its own set of challenges. Juggling between different creative realms demanded immense fidelity and discipline. Lopez's capability to seamlessly transition from one discipline to another speaks to her versatility and turndown to be confined by traditional boundaries, grueling assiduity morals along the way.

Public scrutiny and media attention have been constant challenges throughout Lopez's career. From high- profile connections to critical evaluations of her work, she has faced violent scrutiny under the limelight. still, she has constantly risen above the noise, maintaining focus on her craft and particular growth. Her adaptability in the face of public pressure has come as an alleviation for numerous navigating analogous challenges in the public eye.

In the realm of entrepreneurship, Jennifer Lopez has ventured into colorful business trials, from spices and fashion lines to product companies. Navigating the complications of business in addition to her entertainment career requires strategic decision- timber and a keen understanding of assiduity dynamics. Lopez's success in these gambles reflects not only her creative wit but also her capability to navigate the business geography.

Particular challenges, including high-profile connections and public divorces, have been part of Jennifer Lopez's narrative. still, rather than succumbing to particular lapses, she has employed these gests as sources of strength and growth. Her capability to navigate particular challenges with grace and openness has endeared her to suckers and corroborated her authenticity.

In recent times, the global entertainment geography has experienced significant shifts, told by technological advancements and changing followership preferences. Navigating this evolving geography, Lopez has embraced digital platforms, social media, and new distribution models, staying applicable and connected with her followership. Her rigidity to assiduity changes underscores her life and continued applicability.

In conclusion, Jennifer Lopez's trip is a testament to her adaptability in the face of different challenges. From breaking through assiduity conceptions to managing a multifaceted career and navigating particular and public scrutiny, Lopez has surfaced not only as an entertainment icon but also as a symbol of perseverance. Her capability to navigate challenges, learn from guests , and evolve with the times has solidified her status as a trailblazer in the entertainment industry.

Early Pursuits in Dance and Performance Arts

Jennifer Lopez's early hobbies in cotillion and performance trades laid the root for her multifaceted career as an encyclopedically honored imitator. Lopez demonstrated an early passion for movement and cultural expression.

At the age of five, Jennifer began taking cotillion assignments, marking the commencement of her trip into the world of performing trades. Her parents, feting her gift and fidelity, supported her trials by enrolling her in singing and acting classes, furnishing a well- rounded foundation for her unborn hobbies.

The Bronx, with its vibrant artistic blend, played a vital part in shaping Lopez's cotillion style. told by the different sounds of Latin music, hipsterism- hop, and R&B current in the neighborhood during the 1970s and 1980s, she developed a unique and dynamic approach to cotillion . This emulsion of artistic influences came as a defining element in her performances and contributed to her success in the entertainment industry.

Lopez's early exposure to the performing trades expanded further during her high academy times at Preston High School. Engaging in academy products and continuing her cotillion training, she showcased her versatility and commitment to her craft. These constructive gests set the stage for what would come to be a remarkable career in cotillion , acting, and singing.

A significant advance passed in 1991 when Jennifer Lopez secured a coveted part as a" Fly Girl" cotillion on the popular TV show" In Living Color." This occasion not only showcased her exceptional cotillion chops but also exposed her to a broad followership. The visibility garnered from this part opened doors for farther openings in acting and propelled her towards a career in the entertainment industry.

Lopez's prowess in cotillion continued to shine as she transitioned to acting. In 1995, she delivered a name performance in the biographical film" Selena," portraying the iconic Tejano songster Selena Quintanilla- Pérez. The part needed not only acting but also a deep integration of cotillion , further showcasing her capability to seamlessly combine colorful art forms.

Contemporaneously, Jennifer Lopez ventured into the music industry. In 1999, she released her debut reader," On the 6," featuring a mix of pop, Latin, and R&B influences. The reader's success solidified

her status as a triadic- trouble imitator —
songster, actress, and cotillion .

Throughout her career, Lopez has
continued to incorporate her cotillion
background into her performances,
creating visually stunning and energetic
shows. Her influence in cotillion extends
beyond her particular performances, as
she has also contributed to depleting
cotillion through her part as a judge on the
TV show" World of Dance."

In conclusion, Jennifer Lopez's early
hobbies in cotillion and performance
trades not only reflect her natural gift but
also punctuate the significance of different
influences in shaping her unique cultural
identity. From the cotillion workrooms of

the Bronx to global stages, her trip serves as an alleviation for aspiring players, emphasizing the transformative power of passion, fidelity, and a commitment to cultural excellence.

CHAPTER 3

BREAKING INTO HOLLYWOOD

Jennifer Lopez's rise from the Bronx is a testament to her tenacity, gift, and determination to overcome challenges in pursuit of her dreams. Lopez surfaced from a community that, during the late 20th century, faced profitable rigors, and social struggles, and was frequently overshadowed by negative conceptions.

Growing up in a working-class Puerto Rican family, Lopez's parents, Guadalupe Rodríguez and David Lopez, instilled in her a strong work heritage and adaptability. The Bronx, though scuffling with adversity, handed a rich ground for the development of her artistic identity and cultural bourne. The city's vibrant blend of Latin, African-American, and Caribbean influences came into the background for Lopez's trip to stardom.

Lopez's early guests in the Bronx burned her passion for entertainment. She attended Preston High School, where she continued to hone her chops in singing and dancing. Her intentions led her to Manhattan, where she started taking cotillion classes and worked as a backup cotillion for colorful artists, laying the foundation for her future career.

The breakthrough moment came when Lopez secured a spot as a" Fly Girl" cotillion on the megahit TV show" In Living Color" in 1991. This occasion not only showcased her cotillion prowess but also exposed her to a wider followership. It marked a pivotal turning point, opening doors for acting places in TV and film.

In 1995, Jennifer Lopez landed a commanding part in the film" Selena," portraying the iconic Tejano songster Selena Quintanilla- Pérez. The performance garnered wide sun, establishing Lopez as a talented actress and pelting her into the limelight. Her trip from the Bronx to Hollywood challenged prevailing sundries and came with an alleviation for aspiring artists from underrepresented backgrounds.

Resemblance to her acting success, Lopez ventured into the music industry. In 1999, she released her debut reader," On the 6," featuring map-beating successes like" If You Had My Love." The reader's success solidified her status as a multifaceted imitator, seamlessly blending pop, Latin, and R&B influences.

Jennifer Lopez's rise from the Bronx embodies the spirit of adaptability and determination. Her success not only shattered conceptions associated with her background but also paved the way for lesser diversity and representation in the entertainment industry. Beyond her individual achievements, Lopez remains connected to her roots, using her platform to celebrate and hoist the Bronx, showcasing it as a source of alleviation and strength.

In conclusion, Jennifer Lopez's trip from the Bronx to global stardom is a compelling narrative of triumph over adversity. It underscores the transformative power of the gift, hard work, and a grim pursuit of one's passion, leaving an unforgettable mark on the entertainment geography and inspiring generations to come.

Navigating challenges has been a recurring theme in Jennifer Lopez's outstanding career, reflecting her adaptability, rigidity, and unwavering determination to overcome obstacles. From early struggles in the entertainment assiduity to balancing a multifaceted career, Lopez's trip is a testament to her capability to defy and triumph over challenges.

Beforehand in her career, Jennifer Lopez faced dubitation and rejection, particularly in the film industry . Despite her gift, being a Latina actress posed challenges in an assiduity that, at the time, had limited openings for diversity. Still, Lopez persisted, landing advanced places that defied conceptions and showcased her amusement prowess. Her determination to navigate the hurdles of typecasting and artistic impulses paved the way for lesser inclusivity in Hollywood.

Balancing her places as a songster, actress, and cotillion presented its own set of challenges. Juggling between different creative realms demanded immense fidelity and discipline. Lopez's capability to seamlessly transition from one discipline to another speaks to her versatility and turndown to be confined by traditional boundaries, and grueling assiduity morals along the way.

Public scrutiny and media attention have been constant challenges throughout Lopez's career. From high-profile connections to critical evaluations of her work, she has faced violent scrutiny under the limelight. Still, she has constantly risen above the noise, maintaining focus on her craft and particular growth. Her adaptability in the face of public pressure has alleviated numerous navigating analogous challenges in the public eye.

In the realm of entrepreneurship, Jennifer Lopez has ventured into colorful business trials, from spices and fashion lines to product companies. Navigating the complications of business in addition to her entertainment career requires strategic decision- timber and a keen understanding of assiduity dynamics. Lopez's success in these gambles reflects not only her creative wit but also her capability to navigate the business geography.

particular challenges, including high-profile connections and public divorces, have been part of Jennifer Lopez's narrative. still, rather than succumbing to particular lapses, she has employed these gests as sources of strength and growth. Her capability to navigate particular challenges with grace and openness has endeared her to suckers and corroborated her authenticity.

In recent times, the global entertainment geography has experienced significant shifts, caused by technological advancements and changing followership preferences. Navigating this evolving geography, Lopez has embraced digital platforms, social media, and new distribution models, staying applicable and connected with her followership. Her rigidity to assiduity changes underscores her life and continued applicability.

In conclusion, Jennifer Lopez's trip is a testament to her adaptability in the face of different challenges. From breaking through assiduity conceptions to managing a multifaceted career and navigating particular and public scrutiny,

Lopez has surfaced not only as an entertainment icon but also as a symbol of perseverance. Her capability to navigate challenges, learn from guests, and evolve with the times has solidified her status as a trailblazer in the entertainment industry.

Jennifer Lopez's ascent into Hollywood marked a vital chapter in her outstanding career, reflecting not only her acting prowess but also her tenacity in navigating the competitive geography of the film industry. Lopez's trip to Hollywood was a testament to her multifaceted gift and grim pursuit of success.

Landing Early Acting Roles

Lopez's incursion into Hollywood began with notable early amusement places that showcased her amusement chops and seductiveness. One of her advanced moments came in the biopic" Selena"(1997), where she portrayed the iconic Tejano music artist Selena Quintanilla. The part earned her wide sun and set the stage for her Hollywood elevation.

Solidifying her presence in Hollywood, Lopez starred alongside George Clooney in the crime comedy" Out of Sight"(1998). Her performance as Karen Sisco, aU.S. Marshal, not only demonstrated her on-screen chemistry with Clooney but also garnered critical praise. The film's success further established her as a leading lady in the ensemble.

Lopez showcased her versatility by taking on places across stripes. From romantic slapsticks like" The Marriage Diary"(2001) to crime dramatizations like" Parker"(2013), she demonstrated her capability to attack different characters and narratives. This versatility contributed to her staying power in Hollywood.

Beyond critical sun, Lopez's flicks achieved considerable box office success. Pictures like" Maid in Manhattan"(2002)," Monster-in-Law"(2005), and" Hustlers"(2019) demonstrated her bankability, proving that cults were drawn to her performances across colorful stripes.

Lopez's ascent challenged assiduity morals, especially regarding Latinx representation. Breaking down from stereotypical places, she portrayed complex, empowered characters, showcasing that gift transcends artistic boundaries. Her impact paved the way for increased diversity in Hollywood.

In addition to acting, Lopez ventured into film production. Co-producing flicks like" The Back-Up Plan"(2010) and" Second Act"(2018), she extended her influence behind the scenes, contributing to the creative process and expanding her part in shaping cinematic narratives.

Lopez's trip to Hollywood was stretched with critical sun and awards. Her performance in" Hustlers" garnered wide praise, earning her nominations for prestigious awards like the Golden Globe and Screen Actors Council Awards, reaffirming her status as a reputed actress in the assiduity.

Jennifer Lopez's impact on Hollywood extends beyond individual performances. Her influence on red-carpet fashion, beauty trends, and the overall culture of Hollywood has solidified her status as an artistic icon. Lopez's presence at major events and award shows is eagerly anticipated, reflecting her continuing influence.

Looking ahead, Lopez continues to be a prominent figure in Hollywood with instigative unborn gambles. Whether taking on grueling places, producing compelling stories, or making strides in managerial trials, her ongoing benefactions promise to further shape cinematic geography.

In conclusion, her trip to Hollywood is a testament to her adaptability, gift, and capability to break walls. From her early amusement places to becoming an artistic icon, she has left an unforgettable mark on the assiduity, proving that her star power extends far beyond music and cotillion. As she continues to allure the cult with her cinematic gambles, Lopez remains a force to be reckoned with in the ever-evolving world of Hollywood.

Jennifer Lopez's trip to breaking into Hollywood and landing early acting places is a compelling narrative of continuity, gift, and determination. Lopez's incursion into acting began in a small way that ultimately propelled her into the limelight.

Lopez's early intentions weren't solely concentrated on acting; her original interests leaned towards cotillion and singing. still, as she pursued cotillion training and performed as a backup cotillion for colorful artists, her natural seductiveness and stage presence drew attention. This visibility caught the eye of casting directors, leading to her first amusement openings.

In 1991, Jennifer Lopez secured a career-defining part as a" Fly Girl" cotillion on the popular sketch comedy show" In Living Color." This advance not only showcased her exceptional cotillion chops but also marked her preface to a wider followership. The exposure gained from" In Living Color" served as a stepping gravestone, opening doors for Lopez to transition into acting places.

wharf her first amusement places involved prostrating assiduity challenges, including conceptions associated with her background and gender. Hollywood, at the time, had limited openings for Latina actresses in leading places. still, Lopez's gift and determination defied these constraints.

Her early amusement career gained instigation with places in TV series and flicks. In 1993, Lopez appeared in the TV movie" Lost in the Wild" and landed a guest-starring part in the medical drama" Alternate Chances." These early places allowed her to hone her craft and gain precious experience.

The advance came in 1995 when Jennifer Lopez starred in the film" My Family," directed by Gregory Nava. Her performance as Young Maria garnered critical sun, showcasing her capability to portray complex characters with depth and emotion. The success of" My Family" established Lopez as an able actress, opening doors to more substantial places.

Still, it was her depiction of the iconic Tejano songster Selena Quintanilla- Pérez in the 1997 biographical film" Selena" that pelted Jennifer Lopez to stardom. The film received wide praise, and Lopez's performance earned her a Golden Globe nomination. This part not only showcased her amusement prowess but also demonstrated her capability to embody the substance of real-life characters.

Jennifer Lopez's trip to Hollywood exemplifies the challenges faced by actors breaking into the assiduity, particularly those from underrepresented backgrounds. Her success has not only paved the way for lesser diversity in Hollywood but has also inspired aspiring actors to pursue their dreams against all odds.

In conclusion, Jennifer Lopez's early gests in breaking into Hollywood and landing early acting places emphasize her adaptability, versatility, and commitment to her craft. From the Bronx to the big screen, her trip serves as an alleviation for aspiring artists and stands as a testament to the transformative power of gift and determination in the competitive world of Hollywood.

Challenges and Triumphs in the Film Industry

The film Assiduity is a dynamic and competitive geography where artists encounter a diapason of challenges and triumphs. Jennifer Lopez's trip in the film assiduity exemplifies the adaptability needed to navigate these complications, marked by both lapses and remarkable successes.

Representation and Diversity

Historically, film assiduity has plodded with diversity and representation. Actors from underrepresented backgrounds, like Jennifer Lopez, faced challenges in securing leading places due to assiduity impulses and conceptions.

Typecasting:

This problem, which restricts performers to certain parts based on their race, looks, or prior performance, is common in Hollywood. Actors looking for varied parts may find it difficult to break away from these stereotypes

Gender discrepancies:

For a long time, the film business has struggled with gender discrepancies, which include uneven remuneration and fewer jobs for female performers. It may be difficult for women, particularly those in their forties, to get important and complicated jobs.

Handling Politics in the Industry:

The film business includes complex networks and connections in addition to talent. It may be difficult for both young and seasoned performers to navigate politics, make connections, and get gigs.

Dispelling Preconceptions:

The secret to Jennifer Lopez's success is dispelling the myths surrounding Latina actors. Her performances in movies such as "Out of Sight" and "Selena" showed that she could play a variety of characters while defying expectations and industry standards.

Positive Reviews:

In the film business, winning critical acclaim is a noteworthy accomplishment. Her roles in movies such as "Selena" won her accolades and nominations. Acclaim from colleagues and reviewers strengthens an actor's standing in the business.

Success at the Box Office:

Success at the box office is a concrete indicator of an actor's influence. Lopez's participation in financially successful movies like "Maid in Manhattan" and "The Wedding Planner" proved her star power and capacity to draw crowds.

Producers and Business Initiatives:
Success in the film business goes beyond performing; it also involves role expansion. Jennifer Lopez's accomplishments as a businesswoman and film producer—she co-founded Nuyorican Productions—showcase her capacity to mold stories and influence the artistic direction of the field.

Impact on the Representation:

Triumphs go beyond personal achievement to have wider effects on the industry. The rise in Latina actress representation and the diversification of narratives may be attributed to Jennifer Lopez's impact. Her selections for production show that she is dedicated to promoting inclusion.

In summary, Jennifer Lopez's career in the movie business highlights the contrast between obstacles and achievements. She has become a pioneer, shattering stereotypes and breaking down boundaries in a field rife with prejudice and constraints. Aspiring actors may draw inspiration from her experience, which emphasizes the value of skill, tenacity, and dedication to bringing about constructive change in the film business.

CHAPTER 4

A HARMONIOUS VOICE EMERGES

In the realm of music, the creation of a harmonic voice often denotes the convergence of skill, passion, and commitment. This definition perfectly captures Jennifer Lopez's career, as her melodic voice became recognized in a variety of genres, establishing her as a versatile and significant performer.

Early Investigation into Music:

Jennifer Lopez's early exposure to the variety of sounds in her Bronx neighborhood marked the beginning of her musical career. Her taste in music was influenced by the throbbing energy of hip-hop, the lyrical melodies of R&B, and the rhythmic rhythms of Latin music. The harmonizing voice that would enthrall audiences across the world was founded by these early influences.

1999's "On the 6" debut album:
With her first album, "On the 6," which was named after the subway line she used to travel from the Bronx to Manhattan, Jennifer Lopez made a big splash in the music business in 1999. Her style was characterized by the harmonic synthesis of cultural influences that were shown in the

album, which skillfully combined pop, Latin, and R&B components.

The debut hit, "If You Had My Love," established Lopez as a chart-topping musician in addition to showcasing her vocal prowess. Her voice and the modern production of the late 1990s blended together to create a song that struck a chord with a wide audience and made her a major player in the music business.

Musical Versatility:

The melodic voice of Jennifer Lopez transcends genres. Her flexibility led to her global popularity and solidified her place as a crossover artist. It was obvious when she ventured into Latin music with albums like "J.Lo" (2001), which produced the famous single "Love Don't Cost a Thing.

Top-Charting Achievement:

Lopez's melodic voice dominated charts throughout her musical career. Songs like "Jenny From the Block," "On the Floor," and "Dance Again" demonstrated not just her amazing vocal abilities but also her natural grasp of how the music industry is changing. Working with musicians from other genres demonstrated her versatility even more and added to her long-term success.

Live Acts and Their Locations:

Lopez's melodic voice shines live on stage and is not limited to the recording studio. A mainstay of her career have been her captivating live performances, which are characterized by dynamic dance and strong vocals. Her popular Las Vegas residency, "Jennifer Lopez: All I Have," served as a tribute to her popularity and stage presence throughout time.

Jennifer Lopez is a Latina musician whose melodic voice has greatly influenced how Latin music is portrayed across the world. Her efforts have aided in the removal of obstacles, providing opportunities for Latin musicians and promoting an inclusive music scene.

In conclusion, Jennifer Lopez's melodic voice is evidence of the depth and variety of her musical career. She has created a tapestry of sounds, from the Bronx to international venues, reflecting not just her vocal prowess but also her capacity to cross musical borders and leave a lasting impression on the constantly changing popular music world.

Musical Beginnings and Influences

Jennifer Lopez's musical career began in the Bronx, New York, where the borough's vast cultural variety and her Puerto Rican ethnicity were major influences on her early choices. From a young age, Lopez was surrounded by the rhythmic pulses of merengue, bolero, and salsa, which gave her a strong sense of cultural identity.

Growing up in a loving Puerto Rican family with parents Guadalupe Rodríguez and David Lopez, Jennifer was exposed to both urban Bronx sounds in the 1970s and 1980s as well as traditional Latin music. The borough, which is credited for starting the hip-hop movement, added to the diverse array of musical styles that would eventually shape her sound.

At the age of five, Jennifer Lopez started taking dance classes, which gave her a rhythmic sensitivity that would come in handy for her future musical endeavors. Her parents supported her in her endeavors to pursue acting and singing, which helped her build a strong foundation for her diverse career.

During her artistic career, Lopez drew influence from well-known Latin musicians like as Selena Quintanilla, Tito Puente, and Celia Cruz. Their contributions to world music evolved into significant touchstones that influenced her performing style and shaped her perception of the variety of possibilities found in Latin music.

Beginning her career as a backup dancer for New Kids on the Block, Jennifer Lopez went on to become a "Fly Girl" on the television program "In Living Color" in 1991. This performance not only demonstrated her dancing abilities but also signaled the start of her career in the entertainment industry.

Her first album, "On the 6," which was titled after the subway line that connected the Bronx to Manhattan, was released in 1999 and marked her breakthrough in the music industry. The album presented her as a versatile and crossover musician by skillfully fusing pop, Latin, and R&B genres.

To sum up, Jennifer Lopez's musical roots and inspirations are firmly anchored in her Puerto Rican ancestry, the many sounds of the Bronx, and a genuine admiration for a wide range of musical styles. Her path, which began with her early exposure to well-known Latin musicians and culminated in her first album's blending of ethnic elements, depicts the transformational potential of many musical origins in creating a worldwide music icon.

The Journey to Becoming a Chart-Topping Artist

Jennifer Lopez's path to becoming a top-charting artist is evidence of her versatility, tenacity, and dedication to her creative development. Her journey from a Bronx background to international music fame is characterized by noteworthy turning points and creative rebirth.

Early Life and the Study of Music:
Her early exposure to the variety of sounds in her Bronx neighborhood served

as a springboard for her investigation of music. Coming up in a Puerto Rican family, she was exposed to the rhythms of salsa, merengue, and bolero, fusing her native culture with the urban sounds of the Bronx in the 1970s and 1980s.

Innovation in the Entertainment Industry: Although Lopez was first known for her dancing abilities, her career in show business started in 1991 when she was cast as a "Fly Girl" on "In Living Color." This role not only allowed Lopez to show off her dancing skills but also established her as a prominent figure in the entertainment industry, which paved the way for her eventual transition into music.

1999's "On the 6" debut album:

When Jennifer Lopez's first album, "On the 6," was released in 1999, her musical abilities were brought to light. The title of the record, a reference to the subway line that runs from the Bronx to Manhattan, represented her ascent from humble beginnings to international acclaim. The debut song, "If You Had My Love," demonstrated Lopez's ability to slickly combine pop, Latin, and R&B styles, as it shot to the top of the charts.

Flexibility and Successful Transition:
Her flexibility has been a key component in Lopez's path to becoming a chart-topping performer. She appealed to a wide, global audience while deftly hopping between genres and blending Latin rhythms into her songs. Popular

songs like "Love Don't Cost a Thing" and "Waiting for Tonight" demonstrated her popularity in the crossover arena, reaching the top of music charts throughout the globe.

Significant Partnerships:

Working together was essential to Jennifer Lopez's rise to fame in the music industry. Her chart domination was further cemented when she paired her skills with other famous musicians, such as LL Cool J in "All I Have" and Ja Rule in "I'm Real." These joint ventures demonstrated her versatility while preserving her distinctive tone.

Innovative Stage Presence and Music Videos:

Beyond only her talent, Jennifer Lopez's ascent to the top of the charts was fueled by her captivating live persona and visually spectacular music videos. Famous music videos such as "Jenny From the Block" and "On the Floor" improved the narrative of her songs and further cemented her as a worldwide pop culture icon.

Durability and Significance:

Jennifer Lopez's durability and ongoing significance in the music business are defining characteristics of her career. Her standing as a musical legend with timeless appeal has been cemented by her ability to accept new sounds, adapt to shifting fads, and constantly produce chart-topping singles.

Influence and Recognition Worldwide:

Because of her international adventure, Jennifer Lopez is a worldwide influencer in the music business. Her influence goes beyond her position on the charts; she has shaped discussions about diversity, representation, and how pop music is changing.

In conclusion, a blend of cultural influences, adaptability, and an unshakable dedication to creative quality describe Jennifer Lopez's road to becoming a chart-topping performer. She has had a lasting impact on the music business, pushing a new generation of musicians to strive for greater success, despite her Bronx origins.

CHAPTER 5

Dance, Rhythm, and Global Stardom

Jennifer Lopez's rise to international fame is inextricably linked to dance, rhythm, and her unmatched capacity to enthrall audiences with her captivating performances. Lopez's progression from her early dancing career to her current status as a worldwide celebrity is typified by her remarkable rhythmic abilities and innovative contributions to the entertainment industry.

Early Dance Passion:

Jennifer Lopez started taking dance classes at the early age of five, which marked the beginning of her journey into the world of dance. Lopez was exposed to the rhythmic rhythms of Latin music, hip-hop, and R&B while growing up in the Bronx, a melting pot of many cultural influences. The unique dancing technique that would distinguish her performances was established by this early encounter.

In "In Living Color" (1991–1993), "Fly Girl":
The turning point in Lopez's career occurred in 1991 when she was cast as a "Fly Girl" dancer on the popular television program "In Living Color." This opportunity allowed her to show off her amazing dancing abilities and gain

widespread exposure, which helped her evolve from a dancer into a versatile entertainer.

Change to Music and Acting:

Gaining notoriety from her dancing profession, Jennifer Lopez moved smoothly into acting and music. Her ability to incorporate catchy dance and rhythm into her performances grew to define her as an artist. Her 1999 first album, "On the 6," served as an excellent example of this shift, with dance and rhythm playing significant influences in the creation of the music.

Innovative Choreography:

Beyond only her own shows, Jennifer Lopez has had a significant influence on the dance community. She gained recognition for her avant-garde choreography by working with leading choreographers to produce visually arresting routines. Her dance routines in music videos, like those for "Waiting for Tonight" and "On the Floor," are recognizable because they combine hip-hop and Latin dancing.

Live Performances and Residency Policies:

Lopez's live performances and residencies elevated her mastery of the stage to unprecedented levels. "Jennifer Lopez: All I Have," her Las Vegas residency, featured not just her amazing dancing abilities but also her singing talent. Her continuing vitality and theatrical presence were shown by her performances.

Multicultural Blending in Music Videos:

By fusing elements of her Latina background into her music videos, Lopez achieved a cross-cultural resonance. In addition to honoring her heritage, dance videos like as "Jenny From the Block" and "Let's Get Loud" demonstrated her dedication to diversity and inclusiveness.

The Impact of Television on Dance Culture:

Beyond her roles in stage plays and music videos, Jennifer Lopez has had a significant impact on dance culture. Her influence on the dance world was further cemented when, while serving as a judge on the television program "World of Dance," she developed into a mentor and supporter of up-and-coming dance talent.

Impact on the World and Lasting Legacy:

A lasting legacy has been left by Jennifer Lopez's combination of dance, rhythm, and international fame. Her influence cuts beyond cultural barriers, elevating her to the status of a global inspiration and symbol of empowerment for aspiring actors and dancers.

To sum up, the story of Jennifer Lopez's rise from humble beginnings as a dancer to international fame is entwined with the universal language of dance and rhythm.

She has established herself as a leader in the entertainment industry thanks to her ability to creatively combine cultural elements, create captivating choreography, and enthrall audiences with her performances.

Shaping The Dance Scene With Innovative Moves

Lopez's unique movement style was established at the age of five from her early dancing instruction. She was exposed to a wide variety of rhythms while growing up in the Bronx, including hip-hop, R&B, and Latin music, which contributed to her eclectic background.

Her big break in the dance industry came in 1991 when she was cast as a "Fly Girl" on the television series "In Living Color." This gave her the opportunity to show off not only her technical skills but also her ability to be innovative and creative in the dance form.

With the help of renowned choreographers, Lopez skillfully incorporated her dance background into her musical career, introducing innovative techniques. Because of their avant-garde choreography, music videos such as "Waiting for Tonight" and "If You Had My Love" went on to become classic and redefine visual storytelling.

Her influence was seen not only in music videos but also in her captivating live performances, where her dynamic choreography was a stage staple. From gracing the stages of the world to her Las Vegas residency, "Jennifer Lopez: All I Have," she never failed to wow audiences with her singing and dancing prowess.

Lopez's impact on the dance world has been fundamentally shaped by representation and cultural fusion. She celebrated her roots and helped create a more inclusive representation of dance in the media by skillfully fusing modern choreography with Latin dance forms in her music videos and live performances.

In addition to her work in music, Lopez has had a significant impact on dance as a judge on the television program "World of Dance." She continues to support and promote a variety of dance forms while acting as a mentor and champion for up-and-coming dance talent.

She has received praise and acclaim from all across the world for her inventive choreography, including the 2018 MTV Video Vanguard Award. In addition to her inventive dance routines, Jennifer Lopez has left a lasting legacy that inspires and breaks down boundaries for upcoming dancers.

In summary, Jennifer Lopez's story of dance creativity and creative genius traces her path from the Bronx to worldwide prominence. She is a legendary character whose effect on the dance scene extends beyond music and continues to affect the global creative landscape of dance.

International Impact And Recognition

J. Lopez has left an enduring impression on the world stage, overcoming national and cultural barriers.

Her ability to skillfully combine many cultural elements is the foundation of her rise to worldwide popularity. Raised in the culturally diverse Bronx, she was exposed to the rhythmic pulses of R&B, hip-hop, and Latin music. Her ability to blend cultures became a signature of her work, drawing in viewers from all around the globe.

Lopez's adaptability in a variety of entertainment contexts accounts for her global influence. Her journey into the realms of acting, music, and television has enabled her to establish a worldwide connection with viewers. She has continuously shown a variety of abilities that speak to many cultures, from her chart-topping songs to her critically praised film parts.

On a worldwide level, Jennifer Lopez's music has had unmatched success. Hit songs including "On the Floor," "Let's Get

Loud," and "Ain't Your Mama" have topped worldwide music charts and transcended linguistic and cultural boundaries to become universal hymns.

A global audience is drawn to the visually stunning spectacles that are her music videos. Lopez's graphics, whether they feature dancers against the skyline of New York City or revelers relishing the vivid colors of a Latin carnival, have a global appeal that appeals to individuals of all cultural backgrounds.

Lopez has an effect on the global cinema business. Her performances in films like "Selena," "Out of Sight," and "Maid in Manhattan" have won her praise from critics all around the world and shown her ability to authentically and deeply inhabit a variety of characters.

Jennifer Lopez's impact has grown even further on a worldwide scale via her collaborations with foreign musicians. In addition to topping charts, joint projects with musicians like Pitbull and Wisin y Yandel have promoted cross-cultural understanding by exposing listeners to a variety of musical genres and tongues.

The globe tours and live performances of Jennifer Lopez have played a significant role in establishing her global reputation. Her performances draw crowds from all around the globe, whether they are the main attraction at international events or in renowned venues.

Lopez has a tremendous impact on the fashion and cosmetics industries in addition to the entertainment world. Her reputation as a style icon is well-established worldwide, and her wardrobe selections are praised on red carpets everywhere from Cannes to Hollywood.

Jennifer Lopez's international prominence has been facilitated by her charitable endeavors. Her passion for having a good global influence is evident in her participation in humanitarian endeavors, particularly those pertaining to healthcare and education.

Numerous accolades have been bestowed upon Jennifer Lopez by the global community in recognition of her achievements in the entertainment and artistic fields. Honors such as the MTV Video Vanguard Award and the Billboard Music Awards Icon Award highlight her ongoing impact on a worldwide scale.

In conclusion, Jennifer Lopez's fame and influence around the globe bear witness to her capacity to engage audiences everywhere. She has become a cultural ambassador whose impact transcends national boundaries and enhances the worldwide entertainment scene thanks to her diverse career, success on global charts, and contributions to several sectors.

CHAPTER 6

STYLES AND FASHION EVOLUTION

Jennifer Lopez's design sense and development tell an engrossing story that echoes her rise to international fame. Her early street style, which showcased a propensity for colorful and dynamic fashion choices, highlighted an eclectic blend of cultures and urban energy, emerging from the lively influences of her Bronx childhood.

Lopez's red carpet appearances started to be associated with refinement and glamour as her career took off. She showed off her great sense of style by combining avant-garde designs and traditional shapes with grace at premieres and award presentations.

One of the most pivotal moments in her fashion career was at the 2000 Grammy Awards when she donned a bold Versace gown that hung down beyond her navel. This legendary occasion brought her international recognition and cemented her reputation as a stylish risk-taker.

Beyond the red carpet, Jennifer Lopez's impact could be seen in her music videos, which not only featured her amazing dancing and singing abilities but also established trends in the fashion industry. Her fashion business endeavors, such as the "JLO by Jennifer Lopez" apparel brand, signaled her shift from industry influencer to fashion icon.

Lopez, who collaborates with well-known design companies like Valentino and Balmain, embraced themes with creative and fashionable costumes, attending the Met Gala every year. Her ability to go from Old Hollywood glitz to athleisure chicks shows a self-assured aesthetic that moves between several appearances with ease.

Lopez's impact extends beyond the red carpet and haute couture to streetwear and casual clothing. Her off-duty outfits often combine jeans, bold accessories, and athleisure, giving her an approachable but unquestionably stylish appearance.

Lopez's growth in fashion is characterized by an ageless grace. As she grew older, her style adopted classic and elegant features, defying age-related fashion conventions and encouraging women to see their own beauty in every stage of life.

In addition, Lopez aligns her style choices with her dedication to social and environmental responsibility by using fashion as a platform for charity. She often supports efforts for eco-friendly and sustainable fashion as part of her humanitarian activity.

To sum up, Jennifer Lopez's fashion sense and development show a vibrant journey from the Bronx's streets to worldwide runways. Beyond establishing trends, she has come to represent self-assurance, genuineness, and timeless elegance in the ever-changing fashion industry.

From Fly Girl To Fashion Icon

Jennifer Lopez's extraordinary style progression and unwavering impact in the fashion industry are shown by her remarkable journey from a "Fly Girl" on "In Living Color" to a renowned fashion star. Lopez's rise in the entertainment business has been characterized by her ability to combine streetwear, high fashion, and cultural influences to create a unique and influential personal style.

The Development of the "Fly Girl" (1991–1993):

When Lopez joined the cast of the ground-breaking television program "In Living Color" in 1991 as a "Fly Girl" dancer, she became well-known. Her captivating on-stage persona and captivating dance routines not only demonstrated her abilities but also established the groundwork for her future impact in the entertainment and fashion industries.

As Lopez made the move from dancer to actor, people started to notice her on the red carpet. She adopted an elegant but adventurous style in the late 1990s, hinting at her future as a pioneer in the fashion world. Notably, the dresses and accessories she chose to wear alluded to the role of fashion star she would eventually play.

At the 2000 Grammy Awards, Jennifer Lopez experienced a turning point in her fashion career. With a neckline that hung beyond her navel and a stunning green Versace gown, Lopez wowed the globe and cemented her place as a style legend. She made a risky decision that not only went viral but also cemented her position in red-carpet history as a fashion star.

Jennifer Lopez became a creative in the fashion industry in addition to being a trendsetter. She went into fashion design and started her own clothing brand, "JLO by Jennifer Lopez." This was a change from merely following trends to actively influencing and adding to the business.

Mastery of the Red Carpet and High Fashion Throughout her career, Lopez has always shown her command of the red carpet. She gained recognition for her ability to wear fashionable and imaginative outfits that easily embraced a variety of themes by attending important events such as the Met Gala. Partnerships with prestigious fashion companies like Valentino and Balmain served as further evidence of her impact on the world of high fashion.

Jennifer Lopez is not only seen on red carpets and at prestigious events; she is a true fashion star. Her casual style is just as noteworthy, demonstrating adaptability in embracing fashion without sacrificing a true sense of style. Lopez confidently and seamlessly moves between many trends, from athleisure to casual elegance.

Lopez's style preferences have changed as she has gotten older to appreciate timeless elegance. She defies age and fashion prejudices with her ability to keep a timeless appeal while adjusting to shifting trends, encouraging women to see their beauty at any stage of life.

Beyond aesthetics, Lopez has influenced fashion in the area of charity. Her advocacy for altruistic endeavors often includes using fashion to generate awareness and money. Her style choices are consistent with her dedication to having a good social influence, whether she is supporting sustainability or participating in programs that empower communities.

In summary, Jennifer Lopez's transformation from a "Fly Girl" to a fashion superstar is a story of style advancement, creativity, and pioneering impact. Lopez has not only followed fashion trends but has transformed into a force that defines and molds the always-changing fashion industry via her audacious red carpet-decisions, business endeavors, and dedication to charity.

Influence On Fashion Trends And Brands

Jennifer Lopez's impact on companies and fashion trends is a fascinating story that highlights her standing as a genuine style icon. Lopez is a major influence in creating and establishing fashion trends, and her influence goes far beyond her work in entertainment.

Jennifer Lopez's red carpet revolution is among her greatest accomplishments to fashion. She shot to fame in fashion thanks to the legendary Versace dress she wore to the 2000 Grammy Awards, which became an international sensation. This audacious decision not only immortalized a moment but also established a standard for daring red-carpet fashion statements and taking risks.

Lopez has a special talent for fusing streetwear and high fashion together effortlessly. Her casual outfits, which are often photographed by paparazzi, include denim, striking accessories, and athleisure. Because of its adaptability, streetwear has become a high fashion item, changing the way that manufacturers approach the fusion of comfort and style.

She is a worldwide trendsetter due to her impact which knows no bounds. Her wardrobe selections have a global impact on viewers, igniting trends that spread from Hollywood to other fashion hotspots. She has influenced not only fashion but also haircuts, cosmetics, and general aesthetics, influencing the larger discourse on beauty and style.

Lopez's venture into the fashion industry has made a lasting impression. "JLO by Jennifer Lopez," her clothing business, positioned her as a fashion developer and curator in addition to being a style icon. Her ability to transform personal flair into inclusive, approachable fashion for a wide audience was shown by her endeavor.

Jennifer Lopez's standing in the world of high-end fashion has been cemented by her partnerships with prestigious fashion companies. Collaborations with labels such as Versace, Balmain, and Valentino have shown her ability to slickly combine premium fashion aesthetics with her own style, producing a potent combination.

Lopez has had a big influence on the cosmetics and fragrance industries in addition to the apparel business. Beauty standards have been impacted by her choices in haircuts and cosmetics. Her successful forays into scent lines have further shown her all-encompassing strategy for extending her personal brand into the fashion and cosmetics industries.

Lopez has promoted charity via her influence in fashion. She complements her dedication to social and environmental responsibility with her fashion choices by endorsing eco-friendly and sustainable fashion projects. Her support of using fashion to promote good change increases her influence in the business.

Breaking prejudices and expanding the definition of beauty, Jennifer Lopez is a pioneer for diversity and ethnic representation in fashion. As a result of her advocacy for inclusiveness in the fashion business and her appreciation of her Latina background, industry standards have shifted in favor of more diversity and representation.

Jennifer Lopez's internet presence has increased her popularity in the social media age. She has been able to directly communicate her fashion choices with her followers on social media sites like Instagram, which has enhanced her influence on fashion trends and enabled her to build a dynamic and interactive relationship with her audience.

Jennifer Lopez has left a legacy of classic style that has influenced companies and fashion trends. Her ability to change with the times without sacrificing her genuine, timeless beauty makes her a constant source of inspiration and has a lasting effect on the fashion industry.

In summary, Jennifer Lopez has had a wide-ranging impact on fashion trends and businesses. Her career has been defined by her entrepreneurial endeavors, partnerships with upscale design houses, red-carpet revolutions, philanthropic endeavors, and dedication to diversity and charity. Her influence extends beyond her wardrobe choices; she has completely transformed the fashion business and left her stamp.

CHAPTER 7

JENNIFER LOPEZ'S ROMANTIC AFFECTION AND EMOTIONAL DISTRESS

Despite being well-known, Jennifer Lopez has a private life, which naturally includes love relationships and mental turmoil. I can provide a rough summary of how celebrities, like Lopez, deal with the difficulties of love relationships and the emotional toll that public scrutiny may have as of my knowledge cutoff in January 2022.

Throughout her career, the public has been interested in learning about Jennifer Lopez's love life. She has been in prominent relationships with people in the entertainment world and has been married many times. The media has closely examined every connection, underscoring the difficulties of preserving privacy in the public spotlight.

Lopez's personal life is often the subject of great scrutiny due to her status as a worldwide superstar, which may lead to mental hardship. Rumors, conjecture, and unceasing media coverage may exert a great deal of pressure on prominent figures. It may be emotionally taxing to keep intimate relationships mostly normal while addressing public opinion.

Numerous well-known marriages of Lopez, such as those of Marc Anthony, Ojani Noa, and Cris Judd, have ended in divorce. It may be emotionally draining to navigate the complications of divorce, particularly when doing so in public. Lopez has stressed resilience and personal development while being candid about the lessons she took away from her previous partnerships.

For superstars like Jennifer Lopez, striking a balance between her own pleasure and the demands of the public is a tricky responsibility. Maintaining a public persona while interacting with the public is a continuous struggle, and prominent people often feel emotional anguish as a consequence of this fine balance.

Celebrities often highlight the need for resilience and self-care while dealing with emotional hardship. It becomes essential to maintain mental and emotional health, and many well-known people recommend getting professional help and relying on social networks in trying times.

Personal experiences, such as sexual relationships and emotional suffering, are often expressed in the work of artists such as Jennifer Lopez. Real-life events may serve as an inspiration for songs, movies, and other creative works. This can provide a cathartic release for pent-up emotions and increase the relatability of the works produced.

Lopez has often discussed her own development and maturation, highlighting the lessons she's learned from her former partnerships. Public personalities who experience emotional hardship in the public glare often tell stories of resiliency and personal growth.

Like many other celebrities, Lopez has fought to establish boundaries throughout the years in order to safeguard her private life. Setting boundaries for what may be shared with the public requires conscious attempts to strike a balance between the demands of a public job and a private one.

In summary, while the specifics of Jennifer Lopez's romantic love and personal anguish are naturally personal, the more general difficulties she has when managing relationships in the public view serve as a symbol of the fine balance that superstars must possess. In the world of celebrities, people like Lopez often promote self-care, resilience, and personal development in the midst of these difficulties because they understand the emotional toll that such scrutiny can take.

Jennifer Lopez's High-Profile Relationships

Over her successful career, Jennifer Lopez's love life has unfolded in the limelight, generating public intrigue with her high-profile partnerships. Her path through a number of well-known relationships has been characterized by public scrutiny, media attention, and difficulties preserving one's privacy.

1. Noa Ojani (1997–1998):

Ojani Noa, a model and waitress from Cuba, was the first spouse of Jennifer Lopez. The dissimilarities in their origins attracted attention to their 1997–1998 marriage. Despite the short duration of their marriage, the divorce laid the groundwork for the public's intense curiosity about Lopez's private life.

2. Judd Cris (2001–2003):

The dancer and choreographer Cris Judd was the subject of Lopez's second marriage. Their marriage lasted from 2001 to 2003. They met while shooting her "Love Don't Cost a Thing" music video. Lopez remained the center of attention for the public, particularly as her stature in the entertainment business grew.

3. Ben Affleck, (2002 _2021):

Actor and director Ben Affleck and Jennifer Lopez have had one of the most well-known partnerships in her life. Referred to as "Bennifer" by the press, their involvement in the early 2000s attracted a lot of attention. They resumed their affair in 2021 after a break, beginning a new phase in their partnership.

4. From 2004 until 2014, Marc Anthony:

One of the most significant periods in Jennifer Lopez's personal life was her marriage with singer Marc Anthony. Emme and Max, their twins, were born into their marriage in 2004. The pair's professional partnerships, such as their combined concert series, demonstrated their love of music. But in 2014, their marriage disintegrated.

5. Alex Rodriguez, from 2017 until 2021:

The most recent high-profile relationship that Lopez was involved in was with Alex Rodriguez, a former professional baseball player. Media interest was piqued by their engagement, which was characterized by lavish displays and red-carpet appearances. Regretfully, in 2021, the engagement was called off.

The Difficulties of Public Relations:

Managing well-known partnerships is not without its difficulties. A marriage might experience a great deal of stress due to ongoing public expectations, speculations, and media attention. Jennifer Lopez has recognized on a number of occasions the challenges of keeping one's privacy while one is in the public glare.

Press Coverage and Reporters:

Paparazzi have meticulously tracked Lopez's relationships, examining each public appearance and gesture. Her professional accomplishments have often been eclipsed by the media's fascination with her personal life, underscoring the fine line that celebrities must walk while juggling their personal and public lives.

Impact of the Public on Creative Expression:

Her artwork often reflects the relationships in her life. Some have theorized that songs like "Ain't Your Mama" and "Jenny From the Block" are reflections of her own life experiences. The story that the public hears about her romantic life is further complicated by the confluence of personal connections and creative expression.

Acquiring Knowledge and Development:

Lopez has placed a strong emphasis on personal development and taking lessons from her former relationships, even in high-profile ones. Her capacity to change and use lessons discovered in later relationships is indicative of her tenacity and dedication to self-discovery.

In conclusion, one intriguing facet of Jennifer Lopez's public character has been her high-profile partnerships. Her amorous adventure, which included weddings, engagements, and well-reported reunions, has been extensively covered by the media. Lopez continues to negotiate the intricacies of love in the public glare, providing insights into the difficulties and dynamics of prominent relationships in the entertainment business, even through the highs and lows.

Personal Life Amidst Public Scrutiny

It may be very difficult to manage a private life while under public scrutiny, and Jennifer Lopez is a leading authority on the difficulties of keeping one's privacy while in the public glare. Her path of public romances, marriages, and personal development has been closely watched, emphasizing the fine line that separates the private and public domains.

Jennifer Lopez's rise as an actress, singer, and dancer characterized her early years in the entertainment business. The public's curiosity in her personal life increased along with her notoriety. From her breakthrough performance in "Selena" to her career as a chart-topping musician, Lopez was always in the public eye.

Lopez's love life has been under intense scrutiny, particularly her marriages to Marc Anthony, Ojani Noa, and Cris Judd. The ensuing relationships, including an engagement with Alex Rodriguez, were constantly in the public eye. The media's infatuation with her romances peaked with her engagement to Ben Affleck, dubbed "Bennifer."

It has been difficult to avoid the paparazzi's unrelenting quest of documenting every detail of Jennifer Lopez's private life. Family holidays, private moments, and public activities have all been forced into the public sphere, making it harder to set personal boundaries and creating an atmosphere where privacy is scarce.

Celebrities all know what a negative impact public scrutiny can have on their mental health.

Lopez has spoken candidly about the psychological toll that comes with being watched by the public all the time. There's little question that parts of her mental pain have been exacerbated by the constant criticism of her relationships and the pressure to live up to social norms.

Celebrities often promote self-care and the creation of coping strategies to deal with the difficulties posed by media attention. Jennifer Lopez has emphasized in interviews and public remarks the need to take breaks from the spotlight, get help from professionals, and build a solid support network in order to balance the demands of celebrity.

The need to set and maintain personal boundaries increases when one is the target of constant media attention. Lopez's attempts to keep her family and private life hidden from needless scrutiny highlight how crucial it is to establish boundaries between the public and private selves.

Through creative expression, Jennifer Lopez has found catharsis in the face of public criticism. Her real-life experiences serve as a frequent source of inspiration for songs, movies, and other artistic endeavors, enabling her to reclaim parts of her story and share her viewpoint with the general public.

She has had a good societal effect with her public platform in spite of the obstacles. Through her open discussion of her experiences with scrutiny and her advocacy for mental health and self-care, she adds to the larger discourse on the emotional struggles that people in the public spotlight encounter.

Lopez's resilience is shown by her capacity to change and adapt to the shifting demands of celebrity. She has welcomed personal development and modified her attitude to fame after learning from her previous mistakes, proving that managing a private life in the spotlight requires constant learning and change.

Through her experience living her private life under public scrutiny, Jennifer Lopez leaves a legacy of strength and confidence. Her fortitude, dedication to expressing herself, and support of mental health raise awareness of issues related to mental health and inspire people to put their health first even in the face of the demands of the spotlight.

In summary, Jennifer Lopez's private life under public scrutiny illustrates the delicate balance between privacy and celebrity. Her experiences highlight how crucial it is to establish boundaries, give mental health first priority, and use creative expression as a tool for empowerment. Within the dynamic realm of celebrity culture, Lopez's experience offers an engrossing account of managing personal development while facing public scrutiny.

CHAPTER 8

ENTREPRENEURIAL VENTURES

Through her entrepreneurial endeavors, Jennifer Lopez has shown her adaptability and commercial skills, extending her impact beyond the entertainment industry. Lopez has successfully entered a number of other markets, building a diverse empire that includes fashion, beauty, fragrance, and other sectors.

With the 2001 debut of her apparel brand, "JLO by Jennifer Lopez," she made her foray into the fashion world. A variety of clothing, accessories, and perfumes were offered in the collection. During its active years till 2009, it became a worldwide hit, embodying her style and influencing fashion trends.

The fragrance business has benefited greatly from Jennifer Lopez's influence. She became one of the most successful celebrities in the fragrance industry in 2002 when she launched her first fragrance, "Glow by JLo." This was the start of an empire of fragrances that included several popular smells. Lopez entered the footwear and accessory industries, broadening her influence in the fashion industry. She presented fashionable and varied collections that demonstrated her impact on the fashion and leisure business via partnerships with well-known designers and companies.

In addition to her own business pursuits, Jennifer Lopez is in high demand for collaborations and brand endorsements. Her engagement has strengthened her position as a fashion and beauty star and increased her visibility in the business world. She has endorsed high-end companies and collaborated with mass merchants.

Lopez has achieved great success not just in the beauty and fashion sectors, but also in television production. She is a co-founder of the multimedia business Nuyorican Productions, which has developed and produced a number of television productions, including the popular sitcoms "The Fosters" and "Shades of Blue."

Jennifer Lopez's 2017–2018 venture into reality television as an executive producer and judge on "World of Dance" showed her dedication to helping up-and-coming talent. The program served as a stage for dancers from all around the globe to display their talents, and Lopez's impact on the entertainment industry was further cemented by the show's popularity.

Lopez has expanded her business endeavors into the wellness and health industry. She has used her influence to support holistic well-being via her own lifestyle brand, exercise programs, and partnerships with nutrition companies.

Lopez has embraced the digital era and used social media to interact with her followers and publicize her projects. Her internet presence now forms a crucial component of her business plan as it offers a direct avenue for interaction and marketing.

Strategic investments have been made by Jennifer Lopez, who has partnered with businesses that share her beliefs and brand. Her charitable endeavors also demonstrate a dedication to social responsibility; they include projects supporting healthcare, education, and disaster assistance.

Her support of women in business has also been a defining feature of Lopez's entrepreneurial path. She promotes women's entrepreneurial goals and equality in a variety of fields via her business endeavors and public remarks.

In conclusion, Jennifer Lopez has become a business tycoon with a varied portfolio as a result of her entrepreneurial endeavors. Her ability to move fluidly across multiple industries—from fashion and fragrance to television production and digital engagement—demonstrates not just her commercial acumen but also her flexibility in a

131

constantly changing business environment. Lopez's business accomplishments are motivational, demonstrating that a varied career may go far beyond the theater and cinema.

Fragrance Lines, Clothing, And Beauty Ventures

Jennifer Lopez's influence on the apparel, cosmetics, and fragrance sectors is indicative of her business acumen and diverse mindset. Lopez has effectively transformed her impact in the entertainment industry into a worldwide brand that spans other lifestyle industries.

A pivotal point in Lopez's business career was her foray into the fragrance sector. Her first fragrance, "Glow by JLo," was a huge hit when it was released in 2002. This was the beginning of an empire of fragrances that now boasts a wide range of perfumes, each specially designed to embody different facets of her style and personality. Her perfumes are among the best-selling celebrity scents in the world on a regular basis, demonstrating her popularity and impact on customers.

She entered the fashion business in 2001 when her clothing brand, "JLO by Jennifer Lopez," was introduced. Her own style was reflected in the range, which combined elegance and urban chic. A wide spectrum of clothing, accessories, and shoes was included in the collection, making fashion approachable for a larger group of people. Through partnerships and sponsorships, Lopez has persisted in making a lasting impression on the world of fashion.

Beyond perfumes, the beauty industry has expanded to encompass product lines and partnerships that address skincare and cosmetics. Her beauty projects, which often highlight self-care and overall well-being, demonstrate her dedication to encouraging a radiant and healthy lifestyle.

Her business career has been distinguished by smart alliances with well-known companies. Her collaborations with mainstream stores and endorsements of high-end fashion businesses have increased her prominence in the beauty and fashion industries. These partnerships also demonstrate her ability to fit her style effortlessly into a variety of market niches.

Jennifer Lopez made good use of her social media channels in the age of digital media to interact with her followers and advertise her beauty and fashion endeavors. Her internet presence is a vibrant extension of her business, offering a direct line of contact, a platform for promoting her goods, and a way to interact with a worldwide audience.

Her business ventures have branched out to include holistic lifestyle promotion. She promotes health and wellness via her lifestyle business and provides advice on diet, exercise, and general well-being. Her dedication to leading a healthy lifestyle is consistent with the larger trend of celebrities using their platform to encourage good living.

The apparel, cosmetics, and fragrance brands that Jennifer Lopez has launched have become well-known worldwide. Her brand has an international appeal and connects with a wide range of consumers. Her goods' global success attests to both her marketability and her capacity to engage a diverse range of customers.

Lopez has incorporated social responsibility and charity into her brand in addition to her commercial success. Her passion to have a good global influence is evident in her charity work in areas including healthcare and disaster assistance. Her business endeavors get depth and significance from her socially aware approach.

Beyond only goods, Jennifer has a significant impact on empowering women in the fashion and beauty sectors. She sets an example for prospective business owners in various fields by promoting inclusion, diversity, and empowerment via her accomplishments and activism.

Versatility and invention define Jennifer Lopez's history in the fashion, fragrance, and cosmetics industries. Her capacity to continuously change, adjust to fads, and maintain relevance in fast-paced sectors highlights her business savvy and establishes her as a forerunner in the ever-changing realm of lifestyle companies.

To sum up, Jennifer Lopez's clothes, fragrance, and cosmetics brands perfectly capture her transformation from performer to business tycoon. Possessing an impeccable sense of style, a dedication to excellence, and an international outlook, Lopez has not only established prosperous companies but also emerged as a representation of adaptability and creativity in the beauty and fashion industries.

Business Acumen Beyond Entertainment

Jennifer Lopez's ability to navigate the economic world outside of entertainment is evidence of her adaptability, strategic vision, and spirit of entrepreneurship. Lopez has effectively negotiated a number of sectors, showing a deep comprehension of customer behavior and industry trends.

Her fragrance empire is among the most prominent examples of Lopez's economic prowess. The introduction of her first fragrance, "Glow by JLo," in 2002 signaled the start of an incredibly prosperous career in the cosmetics sector. Being able to produce scents that appeal to people all over the world has made her one of the most prosperous celebrity fragrance entrepreneurs.

Jennifer Lopez's entry into the fashion industry is a prime example of her business portfolio diversification strategy. When the "JLO by Jennifer Lopez" apparel line was introduced in 2001, it became an international hit and highlighted Lopez's unique style. In addition to her own clothing brand, Lopez has strategically collaborated with design businesses, showcasing her ability to negotiate the fast-paced fashion market and her impact in setting trends.

She also dabbles with skincare and cosmetics in addition to scents. Her beauty efforts, which are in line with current trends in the health and beauty industries, stress a holistic approach to well-being. She has been able to effectively adapt her own brand into the lucrative cosmetics sector via product lines and smart collaborations.

Through her co-founding multimedia firm, Nuyorican Productions, she has expanded her business skills to include television production. Through this endeavor, Lopez has expanded her financial interests in the entertainment sector by using her position as a producer, which has been crucial in the creation of popular television programs like "The Fosters" and "Shades of Blue."

She has successfully used her social media channels in the digital age to interact with followers and promote her many endeavors. She offers a direct line of connection, marketing, and brand development with her frequent participation on social media sites like Instagram. Her capacity to adjust to changing trends in customer behavior and communication is shown by this digital interaction.

Jennifer Lopez's brand endorsements and smart partnerships demonstrate her astute business sense. Her alliances boost her marketability and reach, extending from high-end design businesses to general outlets. These partnerships enhance her own brand while demonstrating her capacity to fit in with a variety of market niches.

Lopez has branched herself into the fitness and lifestyle industries in addition to conventional entertainment and fashion. Her exercise regimens and lifestyle brands demonstrate her dedication to leading a healthy lifestyle. Through her alignment with wellness programs, she leverages the increasing consumer interest in living a health-conscious lifestyle.

Her charitable endeavors reveal an entrepreneurial spirit centered on achieving good social change. Her commitment to humanitarian efforts and healthcare and disaster assistance are in line with a socially conscious business strategy. Her whole entrepreneurial brand gains depth and meaning from this dedication.

The success of JLo's businesses throughout the world is evidence of her business savvy. Her capacity to connect with a wide range of people has made it easier for the market to expand internationally. Her awareness of cultural subtleties and worldwide customer preferences is shown by her success on a global scale.

Her commercial impact extends beyond entertainment since she has shown exceptional adaptability. Her company portfolio is vast, ranging from perfumes to clothes, cosmetics, television production, and lifestyle branding. Her capacity to adapt to shifting consumer preferences, seize new business opportunities, and develop a multidimensional brand makes her a leader in the realm of celebrity entrepreneurship.

In conclusion, strategic vision, flexibility, and a comprehensive grasp of several sectors define Jennifer Lopez's commercial acumen outside the entertainment industry. Her success in fragrance, fashion, beauty, television production, and other industries showcases not just her brilliance as an entertainer but also her ability to successfully navigate and shape a variety of business environments.

CHAPTER 9

MULTIFACETED ARTISTRY

Jennifer Lopez is a real entertainment business star thanks to her multidimensional creativity, which includes a broad spectrum of abilities. Lopez has left an enduring impression on the world of culture by flitting between acting, singing, dancing, and business.

Acting was Jennifer Lopez's first venture into the entertainment business. In 1997, she landed her first major part as the legendary singer Selena Quintanilla in the biopic "Selena." This portrayal not only demonstrated her acting abilities but also brought her critical praise and a Golden Globe nomination.

Lopez's entry into the music business confirmed her reputation as a versatile performer. Top singles from her 1999 debut album "On the 6" were the songs "If You Had My Love" and "Waiting for Tonight," which catapulted her to the top of the charts. She kept putting out popular albums, such as "J.Lo" (2001) and "This Is Me... Then" (2002), demonstrating her range as a vocalist and entertainer.

One recurring theme in Lopez's diverse body of work is dance. She has shown remarkable dancing abilities throughout her career, from her early days as a Fly Girl on "In Living Color" to her intense live performances. Lopez's ability to perform in a variety of dance genres, such as

Latin dance and hip-hop, adds to the energy and visual appeal of her shows.

Lopez's diverse artistic abilities extend beyond her work in entertainment to include business. Her beauty products, perfumes, apparel line, and partnerships with other firms all demonstrate a commercial sense that goes well with her artistic pursuits. Her standing as a multifaceted artist is further supported by her capacity to operate in a variety of businesses.

Furthermore, her participation in reality television, namely as a judge on "American Idol" and executive producer/judge on "World of Dance," demonstrates her versatility as a contributor to the entertainment industry. Her commitment to developing new talent is evident in her mentoring and helpful criticism.

Her passion for constructing narratives and sharing a variety of tales is evident in her roles in the production, particularly via Nuyorican Productions. The firm has produced films and television programs, adding to the media's coverage of culture and the larger cultural dialogue.

In residencies and live performances, Lopez's brilliance is on full display. Her ability to command the stage and connect with the audience demonstrates a degree of talent that goes beyond conventional borders, whether she's headlining in Las Vegas or enthralling crowds in sold-out performances.

Her diverse creativity reaches into the world of style and fashion, making her a fashion icon. Her bold wardrobe choices, appearances on the red carpet, and partnerships with designers have had a lasting effect on the fashion business. Beyond only music and movies, Lopez has shaped fashion and established standards for grace and glitz.

In addition to her artistic endeavors, Lopez practices activism and charity, demonstrating her dedication to social problems. Her participation in humanitarian endeavors is indicative of a versatile artist who feels a feeling of obligation to improve society.

The diverse range of Jennifer Lopez's artistic expression is firmly anchored in cultural empowerment and representation. She has shattered stereotypes and cleared the path for more diversity in the entertainment sector as a Latina performer. Her accomplishments highlight the value of empowerment and representation in a variety of creative fields.

To sum up, Jennifer Lopez's many artistic abilities are a vibrant tapestry that combines production, entrepreneurship, dance, music, acting, and activism. Her success in a variety of fields demonstrates a unique blend of brilliance, adaptability, and fortitude, establishing her as a genuine pioneer whose influence extends far beyond the entertainment sector.

Expanding Into Producing And Directing

The addition of producing and directing to Jennifer Lopez's repertoire marks a noteworthy advancement in her diverse career. She has moved from performing, singing, and dancing to assuming important responsibilities in front of and behind the camera, adding to the entertainment industry's creative environment.

The multimedia business Nuyorican Productions, which Jennifer Lopez co-founded with producing partner Benny Medina, marked the beginning of her producing career. Since its founding in 2001, the company—which highlights Lopez's dedication to developing inclusive narratives—has been instrumental in elevating diverse tales to the forefront of cinema and television.

A variety of genres and viewpoints are reflected in the films that Nuyorican Productions has produced. A few examples of Lopez's diverse producing portfolio include "Maid in

Manhattan" (2002), "The Back-up Plan" (2010), and "Hustlers" (2019). Her presence in these productions goes beyond acting, demonstrating her contribution as an artistic force to the development of cinematic narrative.

Nuyorican Productions has had a big influence on television production in addition to movies. In the ever-changing television industry, Lopez has shown her ability to contribute to intriguing storytelling in shows like "The Fosters" (2013–2018) and "Shades of Blue" (2016–2018). Through these initiatives, marginalized voices have been heard and societal concerns have been addressed.

Her move into executive producing is a reflection of her hands-on approach to project development from start to finish. Her passion for creating stories that connect with a wide audience is shown by her participation in the creative process, which includes choosing screenplays, creating plots, and managing production.

Lopez's involvement in reality television as an executive producer and judge adds even more variety to her producing experience. Her directorial debut in "World of Dance" (2017–2018) is a logical step in her career as it demonstrates her capacity to spot and develop talent. She also adds to the show's popularity and broadens her impact beyond written entertainment. As of the deadline in January 2022, to the best of my knowledge, she has not directed a feature picture; yet, her indicated interest in directing parts indicates that she still wants to increase her creative effect and influence in the business.

Through her production activities, Lopez has advocated for an inclusive narrative. By straying from conventional storylines and making a positive impact on a more inclusive and representational entertainment scene, Nuyorican Productions aggressively searches for projects that reflect a varied assortment of viewpoints.

She has actively supported female voices in front of and behind the camera as a well-known personality in the field. Her dedication to giving women in the business opportunity is in line with larger initiatives to eliminate gender disparities in Hollywood.

Jennifer's accomplishments in producing have been acknowledged with nominations and awards. She was an actress and producer on "Hustlers," which received positive reviews, demonstrating her capacity to work on films that appeal to both reviewers and viewers.

The move into directing and producing adds to a long record as a versatile artist. Her versatility in the entertainment sector makes her a pioneer who encourages the next generations of artists and producers to investigate a wide range of creative processes.

In summary, Jennifer Lopez's transition into producing and directing marks a turning point in her professional life. Lopez continues to influence the entertainment industry's narrative via Nuyorican Productions, her dedication to inclusive storytelling, and her possible career as a director. She leaves an enduring impression on the tales conveyed as well as the faces narrating them

Juggling Multiple Roles In The Entertainment Industry

In the entertainment world, juggling several duties is a difficult task. Jennifer Lopez is a shining example of a talent who can handle a variety of obligations with ease. A forerunner in the entertainment industry, Lopez's versatility in acting, singing, dancing, producing, and business has allowed her to do it all.

Following her breakthrough performance as Selena Quintanilla in the 1997 biopic "Selena," Jennifer Lopez's acting career took off. She has since landed a number of parts in movies including "Out of Sight" (1998), "The Wedding Planner" (2001), and "Hustlers" (2019). Her ability to play both tragic and humorous parts demonstrates her flexibility as an actor.

Chart-topping achievements have characterized her music career. From her 1999 debut album "On the 6" to successes like "Jenny From the Block" and "On the Floor," she has shown her abilities as a vocalist and performer by fusing showmanship and dance into her musical performances.

The dancing training Lopez received, first as a Fly Girl on "In Living Color," has continued to be a key component of her professional identity. Her dancing abilities may be seen in live performances, music videos, and even motion pictures such as "Shall We Dance?" (2004). Her reputation as an enthralling performer is partly due to her multifaceted skill.

Lopez has ventured into creating TV series and movies as a co-founder of Nuyorican Productions. She can influence stories, promote inclusive storytelling, and contribute to the entertainment industry as a whole in this capacity. Her role in shows such as "Shades of Blue" and "The Fosters" demonstrates her dedication to diversity narrative.

Among Lopez's business endeavors include a clothing brand, a fragrance empire, and beauty projects. She has succeeded in establishing herself as a fashion icon and entrepreneur by striking a balance between her artistic endeavors and financial savvy. Her adaptability is shown by her ability to move between the entertainment and business sectors.

In reality TV, Lopez has been a judge and executive producer on series such as "American Idol" and "World of Dance." This extra role demonstrates her ability to participate in unscripted formats by offering helpful critiques and guidance to up-and-coming talent.

She uses social media channels in the digital age to interact directly with followers, promote projects, and build connections. Her engaged online persona shows that she is aware of how digital media is changing and how important it is to stay in touch with a worldwide audience.

Lopez has alluded to increasing her involvement behind the camera by expressing an interest in directing. Although she hasn't directed a feature picture as of the January 2022 deadline that I am aware of, her goals in this area suggest that she is always looking to advance and explore her career in the entertainment sector.

Lopez balances several responsibilities in charity as well, regularly participating in humanitarian endeavors. Alongside her entertainment pursuits, her dedication to causes in the fields of healthcare, disaster assistance, and education highlights a sense of social responsibility.

Jennifer's versatility has helped her become well-known around the world. She has had a lasting impression on many different aspects of the entertainment business, from Hollywood to the music charts, fashion runways, and television screens. Her cross-disciplinary impact is evident across national boundaries.

In conclusion, Jennifer Lopez's ability to successfully balance a variety of responsibilities in the entertainment business is evidence of her extraordinary skill, strong work ethic, and flexibility. Her versatility as an artist—singing, dancing, producing, acting, entrepreneurship, and more—positions her as a force to be reckoned with in a variety of entertainment-related fields.

CHAPTER 10

PHILANTHROPY AND ADVOCACY

Jennifer Lopez's dedication to activism and charity highlights her status as a socially aware performer who uses her platform to effect good change. She has actively participated in a number of humanitarian endeavors and has advocated for significant social problems using her platform.

Lopez has participated in a number of healthcare-related projects and has focused her charity on enhancing healthcare facilities and services accessibility. Her efforts have benefited medical facilities and groups advancing patient care and medical research. Lopez has continuously offered assistance with disaster relief initiatives throughout times of need. Her charitable activities have included gathering money and awareness to support impacted areas and offering vital resources for reconstruction and rehabilitation, in the wake of hurricanes and earthquakes.

Lopez has backed programs targeted at improving educational opportunities because he understands the transformational impact of education. Her efforts to empower people via access to high-quality education include a variety of initiatives, including scholarship programs and collaborations with academic institutions.

She also advocates for topics related to child welfare. She has actively participated in campaigns and programs that address the rights of children, especially those that aim to stop child exploitation and abuse. Her voice emphasizes how important it is to provide children with secure and supportive homes.

Lopez has made a strong case for social justice and human rights. Her charitable endeavors include aiding institutions that aim to promote fairness, impartiality, and the safeguarding of essential human rights. Her advocacy is in line with larger movements that aim to create a society that is more inclusive and fair.

Lopez, a well-known woman in the entertainment sector, has supported the emancipation of women. She supports groups that work for women's rights, equality, and opportunity as part of her philanthropy. She helps to establish gender parity and dismantle obstacles via her activism.

Lopez is a pioneer in the entertainment business for Latinos. Her charitable endeavors often support the advancement of diversity in a range of fields and advocacy for Latino communities. She promotes an inclusive society by lending assistance to groups that honor ethnic variety.

In summary, Jennifer Lopez has shown a strong dedication to having a positive influence on a variety of social problems via her activism and charity. Her extensive involvement includes human rights, education, healthcare, disaster assistance, women's empowerment, and environmental protection. Lopez uses her charitable activities as a platform to effect significant change, highlighting the value of empathy, consciousness, and group effort in creating a better society.

Jennifer Lopez's Charitable Contributions

Jennifer Lopez has shown a strong dedication to positively impacting a range of social concerns via her humanitarian initiatives. She has actively supported issues ranging from human rights and education to healthcare and disaster relief by using her platform and resources.

Lopez has continuously supported healthcare efforts by allocating finances and resources to promote patient care, medical facilities, and research. Her altruistic efforts in the medical field have promoted medical breakthroughs and increased access to high-quality healthcare services.

Lopez has always been fast to react to natural tragedies with kind donations. Her humanitarian endeavors include gathering funds for catastrophe assistance, delivering assistance to impacted areas, and endorsing institutions engaged in reconstruction and recuperation endeavors.

Lopez has supported a number of educational projects and organizations because he understands the transformational potential of education. Her philanthropic endeavors often include financing scholarships, instructional materials, and collaborations with establishments to augment educational prospects.

Lopez's philanthropic activity centered on child welfare demonstrates her dedication to the cause of children's rights. She has actively backed groups and initiatives that target problems including child exploitation, abuse, and the general well-being of youth.

As a strong supporter of social justice and human rights, Lopez directs her philanthropic donations to institutions that defend basic rights and build more fair societies. She is in favor of initiatives that encourage diversity and deal with structural inequities.

Lopez is a pioneer for women in the entertainment world, and her charity donations support programs that promote women's empowerment. She is in favor of groups and initiatives that work to improve women's equality, rights, and opportunity in a variety of fields.

She actively supports Latino communities by speaking out in public and giving to charities. She supports programs that honor Latino culture, deal with issues that Latino people experience, and advance diversity and representation.

Lopez has participated in philanthropic initiatives to increase public awareness of HIV/AIDS. Her commitment to tackling global health concerns is shown by her donations to organizations that promote HIV/AIDS awareness and prevention. Her charity donations include programs aimed at environmental sustainability and conservation because she understands the value of environmental stewardship. Her dedication to a comprehensive approach to charity is shown by her support of environmental protection programs.

Lopez had a leading role in relief efforts for the COVID-19 outbreak by actively participating in philanthropic endeavors. Her responses to global disasters were shown by her support of healthcare projects and charity performances that addressed the pressing needs resulting from the epidemic.

Lopez often takes part in and organizes charity galas and fundraising events to raise money for a variety of organizations. Beyond her monetary donations, she actively participates in these events by interacting with the philanthropic community and inspiring people to support initiatives aimed at bringing about good change.

She has partnered with a number of nonprofits, using her platform to help them generate money and exposure. These partnerships show how dedicated she is to fostering long-term support for charities that share her charitable goals and beliefs.

In conclusion, a significant portion of Jennifer Lopez's legacy is comprised of her charity endeavors, which demonstrate a strong sense of obligation to effect good change. Her charitable activities include a broad range of topics, demonstrating a comprehensive strategy for resolving societal concerns and a dedication to using her power for the benefit of society.

Advocacy For Social Causes And Community Empowerment

Jennifer Lopez is a well-known personality in the entertainment world as well as a passionate and committed supporter of good change due to her support of social issues and community empowerment. Lopez has continuously promoted social justice, increased awareness, and strengthened community relationships via her platform.

Lopez grew up in the Bronx and has remained close to her heritage. Her support of community empowerment in the Bronx includes programs that provide locals access to resources, chances for education, and support networks. She has made a strong case for improving the neighborhood that gave rise to her identity.

She fervently promotes educational empowerment because she acknowledges the transformational potential of education. Her projects include funding educational institutions, scholarships, and activities to improve access to education, especially for communities of color. Lopez is an advocate for youth empowerment via projects and programs that connect them with mentors. She has worked on initiatives that inspire, guide, and mentor young people, motivating them to overcome obstacles and follow their aspirations.

Lopez has always supported disaster relief initiatives during trying times. Her dedication to providing prompt assistance and support to communities impacted by calamities or natural disasters is shown by her participation in relief efforts and fundraising drives.

A strong supporter of justice and equality, Lopez is an outspoken campaigner for human rights. Her public remarks and charitable endeavors support issues that deal with prejudice, systematic injustices, and the goal of equal chances for all people, regardless of identity or background. Lopez is a prominent Latina who fights for Latinos' representation and rights. Her projects center on dispelling myths, advancing cultural diversity and making sure that Latinos are fairly represented in a range of fields, such as politics, business, and entertainment.

Lopez is an advocate for women's empowerment and gender equality. Her involvement includes backing programs that promote diversity, combat gender inequality, and provide women chances in both conventional and non-traditional sectors.

Lopez supports the preservation and celebration of many cultural heritages because he understands how important it is to preserve culture. Her efforts are directed at making sure that cultural customs are honored, maintained, and transmitted to the next generations.

Lopez has participated in anti-bullying initiatives and used her platform to spread the word about the negative impacts of bullying. Her activism seeks to promote empathy and understanding in order to make places safer, especially for kids and teens.

Her activism encompasses public health efforts that support illness prevention and healthy lives. Her passion for resolving health inequities and her holistic approach to community well-being are evident in her engagement in health-related initiatives.

Lopez promotes sustainability and environmental stewardship because he understands how urgent environmental concerns are. Her actions include endorsing initiatives and campaigns that tackle climate change, save the environment, and encourage environmentally responsible behavior.

Lopez strongly promotes civic involvement and voting turnout. She advocates for programs that boost voter participation, particularly in marginalized areas. She wants to provide people the ability to influence the direction of their communities and civilizations by encouraging civic engagement.

In conclusion, JLo demonstrates a multidimensional dedication to bringing about good change via her engagement in social concerns and community development. Her advocacy work encompasses a broad range of problems, from environmental stewardship and education to human rights, cultural representation, and education. This reflects a comprehensive approach to having a significant influence on society.

CHAPTER 11

RESILIENCE IN THE SPOTLIGHT

The limelight resilience that Jennifer Lopez has shown throughout her remarkable career is a testimonial to her persistent tenacity, flexibility, and capacity to overcome adversities. She has shown an incredible tenacity that goes beyond her jobs as an actor, singer, and dancer as she has negotiated the ever-changing entertainment business.

Lopez's path started in the tough Bronx, where she had to deal with financial difficulties. Her love of the performing arts and her desire to succeed in the entertainment business inspired her to persevere through hardship and follow her dreams despite the challenges.

Lopez had early difficulties entering into Hollywood, a mostly white business at the time, as a Latina performer. Her tenacity was evident as she persisted, landing parts that highlighted her abilities and dispelled prejudices, finally opening the door for further diversity in the entertainment industry.

Her ability to move between acting, singing, dancing, producing, and business with ease is a testament to her tenacity. Adopting a multifarious profession, she has adeptly navigated several roles, exhibiting adaptability that surpasses conventional entertainment conventions.

She has endured harsh media scrutiny and criticism throughout her career, especially with regard to her relationships and personal life. She has remained committed to her work despite being in the public eye, showing fortitude in the face of unrelenting scrutiny and criticism.

Lopez has seen both periodic disappointments and chart-topping success in his music career. Her capacity to bounce back, adapt her sound, and maintain her position as a strong force in the music business is clear, as she has done so from the heights of her first album "On the 6" to times of critical review.

Over the years, the entertainment sector has seen tremendous changes, including the emergence of digital platforms and shifting customer tastes. Lopez's ability to adjust to these changes in the business, embrace new platforms, interact with her fans on social media, and maintain her relevance in a constantly changing environment are all examples of her resilience.

It may be difficult to juggle a hard profession and personal life, particularly when it's in the limelight. Lopez's ability to keep relationships harmonious, manage her personal and professional lives, and project a favorable public image are all examples of her resilience.

There were business hurdles associated with Lopez's entrance into entrepreneurship, which included her apparel lines, fragrance empire, and cosmetic endeavors. She effectively establishes herself as a business entrepreneur by navigating the difficult worlds of fashion, beauty, and lifestyle, demonstrating her tenacity in the business world.

She has had difficulties as an actor because of typecasting and the dearth of roles available to Latina actresses. Her passion for diversity in cinema and her proactive attempts to get parts that defy prejudices, contributing to increased representation on screen, exemplify her resilience.

Lopez's capacity to bounce back from job losses, personal obstacles, or negative evaluations highlights her tenacity. Her ability to grow from experiences, reinvent herself, and bounce back from losses is a testament to the tenacity that has been her trademark in the business.

Her rise from the Bronx to the stature of a worldwide superstar illustrates her tenacity on a large scale. She has become not just a cultural icon but also a symbol of perseverance, encouraging generations of artists to follow their aspirations despite hurdles and expectations.

Lopez's tenacity is seen in her charitable activities in addition to her profession in entertainment. Her dedication to social concerns and support of constructive change demonstrates a fortitude based on a want to have a significant influence outside of the limelight.

In summary, resilience in the limelight is an inspiring tale of overcoming adversity. She represents the spirit of resilience—adapting, overcoming, and prospering in a field that needs ongoing evolution—from her early days in the Bronx to her achievement of worldwide fame. Aspiring artists may draw inspiration from

Lopez's path, which also demonstrates the lasting value of perseverance in pursuing one's hobbies.

Overcoming Career Challenges

Jennifer Lopez's story of perseverance, tenacity, and flexibility in the face of professional obstacles is a riveting read about her path in the entertainment world. Throughout her career, Lopez has faced and overcome many challenges, making a name for herself as a multidimensional figure in Hollywood and beyond.

In the beginning, Lopez had trouble becoming well-known for his performances. Even with acting and dancing expertise, it was difficult to enter into the business. She persevered through little parts and auditions, unfazed, setting the groundwork for her persistent strategy to overcome obstacles in her career.

Lopez faced cultural obstacles in Hollywood, where diversity was scarce, as a Latina performer. She successfully handled obstacles by choosing positions that went against expectations, shattering preconceptions and industry conventions in the process, and opening doors for more diversity.

There was doubt about Lopez's rise from a background dancer to a reputable actor. Although others questioned her capacity to go beyond her dance image, she accepted the challenge. Her breakthrough performance as Selena in the 1997 film "Selena" dispelled skeptics and demonstrated her acting talent.

Getting into the music business was another challenge. There was skepticism when she switched from acting to singing. But Lopez's 1999 first album "On the 6" not only silenced her detractors but also catapulted her into music fame by proving her tenacity and capacity to overcome doubt.

Her public image suffered as a result of the media's continuous probing of her personal life. She persevered in the face of external pressures to her job, demonstrating a remarkable capacity to compartmentalize and stay focused despite personal issues and heavy tabloid attention.

Lopez had success at the box office, but she also had significant difficulties playing specific parts in movies. She proceeded to take on a variety of projects while juggling the demands of both critical and economic success, exhibiting tenacity in her dedication to creative inquiry.

There were entrepreneurial hurdles while starting apparel lines, perfumes, and cosmetics businesses. Lopez's ability to overcome obstacles, grow from failures, and create profitable brands—all of which have helped her establish herself as a shrewd business woman—demonstrates her resilience in the business world.

Throughout his career, Lopez has experienced comebacks and periods of reinvention. She purposefully remade herself, from breaks from music to cinematic endeavors that altered her image. She demonstrated an adaptable strategy to get over a rut and stay relevant in the rapidly changing entertainment landscape.

Actresses have faced obstacles as they age due to Hollywood's ageism. But Lopez defies age stereotypes, landing big parts and continuing to have an impact. Her willingness to defy accepted practices in the industry shows her fortitude in the face of age-based prejudice in the entertainment industry.

For artists, juggling rigorous work with a family life is a frequent difficulty. Lopez's ability to strike this balance demonstrates her tenacity and emphasizes how important it is to put personal ties first even while pursuing success in a well-known field.

Lopez had to deal with the difficulties of being a trailblazer in the field of Latinx representation. She aggressively promotes diversity, breaking down barriers for upcoming Latinx performers and creating a more welcoming entertainment environment.

By using her platform for charity, Lopez finds ways to transform obstacles into possibilities. Her commitment to philanthropic causes gives her a purpose outside of the entertainment industry and demonstrates her tenacity in changing social challenges.

In summary, Jennifer Lopez's story shows how to overcome obstacles in your profession with poise and tenacity. She has consistently changed, remade herself, and bucked business conventions despite her early hardships and Hollywood's mistrust of her. Lopez's narrative encourages budding artists to persevere through the difficulties of navigating the entertainment business, serving as a reminder that setbacks may serve as stepping stones toward long-term success.

Maintaining Relevance Across Decades

Jennifer Lopez's remarkable skill, astute judgment, and flexibility in the ever-changing entertainment sector are the reasons for her ability to remain relevant over many decades. Lopez has become a worldwide icon after making a smooth transition from a background dancer to one of Hollywood's most powerful people.

Her continued significance may be attributed in large part to her versatility as a singer, actress, dancer, and businesswoman. Her versatility has made her appealing to a wide range of viewers and helped her maintain her status as a well-known personality in a number of entertainment industries.

Lopez's continued relevance may be largely attributed to her astute professional decisions. With notable performances in films like "Selena" (1997), popular songs that reach the top of the charts, and captivating TV appearances, she skillfully varies her endeavors to maintain a wide-ranging and steady public profile.

Her enduring significance has been aided by her role as a worldwide symbol. Her impact transcends national boundaries and reaches global audiences. Through successful movies, international tours, and partnerships with well-known companies, she has established a brand that is familiar to everyone.

In order to be relevant, one must adjust to changes in the business, and Lopez has shown that she is capable of adopting emerging trends and technology. She remains in touch with her followers and navigates the ever-changing media consumption environment by using digital marketing and social media channels.

Lopez's continuing appeal has been greatly influenced by her ability to change her appearance. With her "Jenny From the Block" character and her glitzy red carpet appearances, she skillfully handles changes in public opinion while clinging to her true self, which keeps her image captivating and new.

Her influence on style and fashion has greatly increased her importance, and her red-carpet and off-the-red-carpet appearances have elevated her to the status of a fashion icon. Her impact in the ever-changing world of style is shown via her partnerships with designers and the introduction of her own fashion lines.

Lopez's continued relevance has been greatly aided by her steady success in the music business. Top-charting singles like "On the Floor" and "Dance Again" show that she can remain relevant and appeal to modern listeners' interests in music.

Posing as a shrewd businesswoman, Lopez has made a name for herself in the fashion, fragrance, and cosmetic industries. Her business endeavors demonstrate her capacity to excel in a variety of areas and enhance her overall brand.

By using social media sites actively, Lopez has been able to establish a direct connection with her fans. Her social media presence makes her more approachable and keeps her followers interested, whether she is promoting projects or giving behind-the-scenes looks into her life.

A careful balance between financial success and creative integrity is needed to be relevant. Lopez has skillfully struck this balance by taking on parts that highlight her acting abilities and working on successful projects that appeal to a larger audience.

Lopez's effect on trends, memes, and allusions in popular media is indicative of her cultural influence. With her recognizable green Versace outfit and words like "JLo Glow," she has made a lasting impression on popular culture.

In summary, Jennifer Lopez's longevity in the business may be attributed to a variety of elements, including her diverse skill set, astute professional decisions, flexibility in response to changing market conditions, and a well-manicured public persona. Lopez is a pioneer and innovator who has captivated audiences all around the globe and left a lasting impact in the entertainment business that goes beyond time and cultural upheavals.

CHAPTER 12

CONTINUING THE LEGACY

A complex and significant part of Jennifer Lopez's career and influence on the entertainment business is carrying on their heritage. Lopez has had a lasting impression on culture in addition to her own enormous success and her role as a trailblazer for subsequent generations.

One aspect of her legacy is that she paved the way for Latinx representation in Hollywood. She has broken down barriers and provided opportunities for other Latinx musicians, demonstrating that creativity is not limited by cultural boundaries. A new wave of inclusion in the entertainment business has been spurred by her popularity.

Lopez is a worldwide cultural figure whose influence endures. Her effect is felt by a wide range of people worldwide because of her influence on fashion, music, and movies. She has left a lasting impact on the global scene and has come to represent empowerment and resilience.

Her flexibility and multidimensional skills form the foundation of her legacy. She has shown a unique blend of abilities in acting, singing, dancing, and business. Her success in a variety of disciplines has established a benchmark for artists looking to broaden their horizons.

One of Lopez's lasting legacies as a proponent of diversity and inclusivity is her outspoken position on the value of representation. Her influence on the fashion and beauty sectors adds to her lasting legacy. She has aggressively championed equitable opportunity for people from all backgrounds via her business and charity, changing industry norms. With her lucrative fragrance lines, red-carpet appearances, and partnerships with well-known designers, she has shaped fashion trends and made a name for herself in the beauty and fashion industries.

Possessing a solid business background, Lopez has gone into the clothes, fragrance, and beauty product industries. Her business sense goes beyond entertainment, serving as a role model for artists looking to build their brands across a range of sectors.

Lopez's dedication to social impact and generosity will live on in her legacy. Her participation in a number of humanitarian endeavors demonstrates her passion to change the world for the better. She leverages her influence to inspire people to make contributions to worthwhile causes.

Her ability to maintain a high-profile work and a family life is a significant part of Lopez's legacy. She is a role model for those who are juggling their personal and professional lives, showing that achievement and a happy family life can coexist.

Future generations of artists may draw inspiration from Lopez's legacy. Her ascension from the Bronx to international fame serves as an example of what can be achieved with perseverance, hard effort, and a steadfast faith in one's own ability.

Lopez's continued relevance and flexibility are essential components of her legacy. She maintains her relevance and influence in the rapidly evolving entertainment sector by keeping abreast of changes in the industry, adopting new technology, and reinventing herself as necessary.

She has received many honors and recognition across the world, including significant acting prizes and Grammy nominations, for her contributions to the arts, which have been acknowledged on a worldwide scale and cemented her position in entertainment history.

Lopez's commitment to mentoring and educational endeavors has contributed to her legacy. She contributes to the growth of prospective artists via mentoring programs and scholarships, making a long-lasting influence on the next generation of gifted people.

In summary, Jennifer Lopez's legacy is a complex web that includes her contributions to philanthropy, her business endeavors, her advocacy for diversity and inclusion, and her accomplishments in entertainment. Through persistently pushing limits and motivating others, she solidifies her status as a transformational character whose influence goes far beyond her own achievements. Her story is a lighthouse for individuals who want to make a significant difference in entertainment and other fields.

Jennifer Lopez's Ongoing Projects And Future Endeavors

Jennifer Lopez has played parts in a wide range of genres over her extensive career in the film business. Future and ongoing endeavors may include new film partnerships, in which she might portray a variety of characters, demonstrating her acting range. Keep an eye out for information about her participation in forthcoming motion picture projects.

Lopez probably keeps trying her hand at different musical endeavors because of her prosperous musical career. This might include the publication of brand-new albums or singles, or even taking part in artistic partnerships. For information on forthcoming releases, follow her on social media and via updates from her record company.

She has worked as an actor and a producer on television shows. Her next projects might include producing her own creations, making guest appearances on television, or even creating new series. For possible TV shows, keep an eye out for announcements from networks and streaming services.

Possessing a significant presence in the business sector, Lopez could be able to grow her company. This might include the introduction of new fragrances, fashion collections, or creative commercial ventures. Watch this space for updates on her partnerships and business ventures.

Because of Lopez's dedication to charity, she could continue to support different organizations in existing and future initiatives. This might be working with nonprofits, hosting fundraising activities, or starting new projects to deal with social concerns.

Jennifer Lopez is well-known for having a big impact on the beauty and fashion sectors. Keep an eye out for any upcoming product launches under her name or partnerships with designers or cosmetics businesses. Her influence on beauty and fashion trends is probably not going to go away.

If it's possible, Lopez may start doing live shows and tours. This can include performances of her choreography and musical repertory at concerts. For information on any upcoming tours, pay attention to announcements made via her official channels.

She may still take on high-profile acting roles given her reputation in the business, perhaps in big-name TV shows or movies that attract a lot of attention. Her next acting ventures will be revealed via updates on casting calls and movie releases.

Jennifer Lopez has a track record of forming noteworthy alliances and partnerships. Future projects can include collaborating with businesses, influencers from other sectors, or other artists. Watch for news about possible projects that highlight her wide range of skills.

In keeping with her tradition of helping up-and-coming artists, she may contribute to educational projects and mentoring schemes.

These might include grants, seminars, or chances for mentorship for those who want to work as artists.

The Everlasting Impact On The World Of Entertainment

The enduring influence Jennifer Lopez has had on the entertainment industry is proof of her diverse skill set, tenacity, and ground-breaking work in the fields of music, cinema, fashion, and business. She has created a legacy in New York that will last for years, making her a universally recognized figure.

She has paved the road for more representation and broken down boundaries based on culture in the entertainment industry. She broke through prejudices as a Latina musician and became a pioneer, providing a platform for many views in an industry that had not always been inclusive.

Her enduring influence has been largely attributed to her artistic diversity. Lopez demonstrated a unique blend of abilities that has distinguished her as a genuine performer as she moved from acting to singing and dancing with ease.

Chart-topping tracks have defined Lopez's music career and shown her dominance in the music industry. Not only did songs like "If You Had My Love" and "On the Floor" soar into the charts, but they also became universally recognized anthems.

Lopez is a fashion star whose influence is seen in the fields of beauty and fashion in addition to entertainment. Her bold design choices—such as the classic Versace green dress—have set trends, and her successful forays into fragrance and fashion lines have cemented her position as a major player in the beauty business.

Her success at the box office and acting abilities have greatly influenced her influence in the movie business. Her noteworthy roles in movies such as "Out of Sight," "Selena," and "Hustlers" have won her praise from critics and shown her versatility as an actor.

Her success as a businesswoman has extended her reach beyond the stage and screen. Her forays into apparel brands, perfumes, and cosmetics have not only brought her success on the market but also shown her to be an astute entrepreneur.

Lopez's influence is a worldwide cultural phenomenon that is not limited to any one area. Her global viewership makes her a symbol of inspiration and empowerment for people from a wide range of backgrounds. She has had a significant influence on pop culture. Her impact may be seen in memes, pop culture allusions, and everyday discussions in addition to her creative output. A few instances of her enduring influence on popular culture include the "JLo Glow" and her influence on red carpet culture.

Lopez has used social media to communicate directly with her followers in the digital era. Her frequent use of social media sites like Instagram enables her to interact with followers, provide behind-the-scenes photos, and maintain her relevance in the rapidly changing media world.

Her tenacity and fortitude also characterize her legacy. She is an inspiration for handling the difficulties of celebrity with poise and tenacity, having overcome obstacles in the profession, negative media attention, and personal disappointments.

Lopez has a philanthropic influence as well, utilizing her position to support a range of humanitarian concerns. She has actively participated in changing the world for the better, whether it is by promoting social justice, education, or disaster relief. Her influence will last forever since she serves as a model for the next artistic generations. Her climb to fame on a worldwide scale from the Bronx is proof of the potential that can be realized with skill, perseverance, and a steadfast dedication to one's goals.

In summary, Jennifer Lopez's enduring effect on the entertainment industry is a complex fabric made of her creative talent, cultural clout, commercial savvy, and dedication to good change. As a universal symbol, she keeps influencing the entertainment industry and motivating others to pursue their goals, establishing a lasting legacy that is felt all over the globe.

Inspirational Takeaways For Readers

Examining Jennifer Lopez's life and work offers readers various motivational lessons that go beyond the entertainment sector. Readers may learn the following important lessons from her journey:

1. Unwavering Willpower:

Lopez's story serves as an example of the strength of steadfast resolve. She overcame several obstacles in her quest for achievement, from her early years in the Bronx to her rise to international fame. Her perseverance in overcoming setbacks and remaining dedicated to her objectives might serve as an encouragement to readers.

2. Adaptability and Versatility:

One of the most important lessons from Lopez's career is the capacity for adaptation and variety. She exemplifies the value of adaptability in a dynamic and changing environment by juggling acting, singing, and dancing as well as pursuing business.

3. Shattering Cultural Barriers:

Lopez's contribution to tearing down barriers between cultures emphasizes the value of variety and representation. Readers may be motivated to question accepted wisdom, push boundaries, and help build a more varied and inclusive society by doing so.

4. Maintaining a Healthy Work-Life Balance:

In Lopez's path, striking a balance between personal and professional life has been a recurrent subject. Readers may get insight from her example of balancing the demands of celebrity with meaningful connections and putting one's own well-being first.

5. Empowering Entrepreneurs:

Lopez's entrepreneurial success highlights the possibility for both business savvy and self-empowerment. Readers are encouraged to investigate business opportunities, take measured risks, and develop their brands outside of conventional job trajectories.

6. Adaptability in the Face of Adversity:

One important lesson to be learned from Lopez's experiences is the capacity to withstand criticism and media attention. Her ability to rise above hardship and concentrate on personal development and creative expression might serve as an example for readers.

7. Global Effects and Social Duty:

Lopez's dedication to social concerns and charity emphasizes how crucial it is to utilize influence to bring about good change. Readers may be motivated to address social concerns by using their position to push for reform and have a significant influence on their local communities.

8. Building a Robust Work Ethic

Lopez's success stems from her commitment to her profession and great work ethic. In order to achieve long-term objectives and consistent achievement, readers may understand the importance of perseverance, discipline, and hard effort.

9. Accepting Reimagination:

Throughout Lopez's professional life, the idea of reinvention has been present. By embracing change, looking for new chances, and reinventing oneself when needed, readers may be inspired to improve both personally and professionally.

10. Motivating Upcoming Generations:

Future generations may draw inspiration from Lopez's path. The significance of leading the example for others, actively promoting diversity, and having a good impact on those who look up to you may be instilled in readers.

In conclusion, readers may learn a great deal of inspiration from Jennifer Lopez's life and profession. Her story inspires those who want to leave their impact on the world, whether it is via social duty, resilience, adaptation, or pursuing a variety of hobbies.

Conclusion

As the fascinating JLo Unveiling draws to a conclusion, we are once again engrossed in the incredible journey of a lady who goes beyond the entertainment industry to become a timeless representation of diversity, tenacity, and unwavering desire. Lopez's journey, which took him from the colorful slums of the Bronx to the glamorous stages of Hollywood, is more than just a biography of celebrity; it is a monument to the unwavering spirit that makes dreams come true.

The deep effect of her cultural influence, the reverberations of her hit songs, and the striking memories of her legendary performances linger with us long after we turn the last page of this book. Lopez's story is more than just a tale of achievement; it's a mosaic of lessons learned about overcoming obstacles, going against the grain, and appreciating the beauty in one's own individuality.

The common thread that runs through her life—a story of perseverance, self-reinvention, and the unrelenting pursuit of passions—resonates deeply. The life story of Jennifer Lopez is a source of motivation for aspirants, a handbook for negotiating the difficulties of celebrity, and a celebration of the endless opportunities that result when sincerity and drive combine.

We take with us the song of her journey—the highs and lows, the symphony of a life lived fearlessly—as we say goodbye to the pages that reveal the intricacies of this multidimensional artist. Jennifer Lopez's biography is a glittering thread in the vast tapestry of the entertainment industry, adding to the rich tale of people who dare to dream, persevere in the face of adversity, and make a lasting impression on the stage of life.

www.ingramcontent.com/pod-product-compliance
Lightning Source LLC
Chambersburg PA
CBHW072150290526
45794CB00004B/1465